"As I read this book, in one sitting, ... d to give a copy to: my daughter, my sons, n ... .I could just see how their lives would be enr ... neously, through this beautiful collection of stc ... a sense of sisterly pride and gratitude, since several of tl ... are my friends and colleagues. I have personally experienced the power of their support, and I know how their ways of being in relationships, full of curiosity and appreciation, can discover possibilities that were undreamt of before. I am excited in anticipation of how the combined brilliance, generosity and skills of the authors of *Thriving Women Thriving World* will help many people have fuller lives and greater well-being, all over the world."

–Margarita Tarragona, Ph.D. President, Mexican Positive Psychology Society
Co-founder, Grupo Campos Elíseos

"This masterful guide provides an honest yet positive path forward for women who have suffered and those who love them. Its adept appreciative inquiry questions invite learning, compassion and world changing actions. Prophetic in voice, compassionate in tone, it is a true treasure. The world needs this book."

–Amanda Trosten-Bloom, Principal, Corporation for Positive Change
Author, *The Power of Appreciative Inquiry*

"What an amazing and inspiring resource Diana Whitney, co-authors, and contributors have created! Talking about what bothers us is easy. We do it all the time. Rarely do we stop and ask ourselves what we would *like* to see in our relationships and ourselves – what would bring joy and connection. This book is jam-packed with creative resources that invite us to reflect on what we value, what we want more of, and how we can engage with others to create these thriving spaces."

–Sheila McNamee, Ph.D. Vice President, Taos Institute
Professor of Communication, University of New Hampshire

"Filled with questions that represent a wise and generative call to action for empowering thriving women for a thriving world. A book for our times and essential reading for us all!"

–Marilee Adams, Ph.D. Author, *Change Your Questions, Change Your Life*

Thriving Women Thriving World unfolds virtually all areas within the female and female-identifying perspective, encouraging explorative dialogue into what was, what is, and what could be in this critical stage of the feminist movement. Diana Whitney and her coauthors share historical background, and then a treasure-trove of carefully designed Appreciative Inquiry questions around these topics, enabling groups of people to enter into critical dialogue in any number of settings, such as social clubs, advocacy groups, professional gatherings, and so many others….in order to unwrap and explore these sometimes sensitive subjects, share stories, and together design new possibilities for moving forward. I was awestruck as to the myriad of applications for this work and inspired to run out and gather a group to get started!

–Fran Lyon-Dugin, Ph.D. Faculty, Augsburg University
and Taos Institute Associate

Thriving Women Thriving World is a treasure chest of stories and artistry to raise-up conversations around women's empowerment. It is an important resource to bring more self-love, connection and wisdom to women's lives, creating a positive ripple on our world.

–Kami Guildner, Business Coach for Women, Author, *Firedancer*
Founder and Host, *Extraordinary Women Radio*

"In this provocative book, *Thriving Women Thriving World*, Diana Whitney and co-authors invite us to tell our own stories – new stories, infused with hope and positive possibilities. Using the positively deviant practice of Appreciative Inquiry, Diana and company nudge us to turn the #MeToo movement inside out to catalyze inspiring dialogue and much-needed change. If you're looking to find new energy to solve age-old and often tiresome problems surrounding gender inequality, this book stands to be an excellent guide."

–Barbara L. Fredrickson, Ph.D. Author of *Positivity* and *Love 2.0*
Kenan Distinguished Professor, University of North Carolina at Chapel Hill

As Mary Gergen notes in the foreword, Diana Whitney and her colleagues put forth a refreshing and challenging approach to gender issues: *appreciation rather than aggression*. They speak to the remarkable potential for new understandings and ways of living 'gender issues' that an appreciative perspective and action offer – with enormous benefit for all.

–Harlene Anderson, Ph.D. Co-founder, Houston Galveston Institute
and Taos Institute

This book explores the notion of a world where women thrive. It provides an opportunity to take part in creating that world. A wide range of topics are explored with insightful questions that the reader can employ to engender meaningful conversations. The vignettes spoke to me of a world of thriving women that already exists, forming the foundation of a future where all of us, regardless of gender, will thrive.

–Bonnie Milne, Ph.D.

Thriving Women Thriving World

AN INVITATION TO DIALOGUE, HEALING, AND INSPIRED ACTIONS

Diana Whitney

Jessica Cocciolone

Caroline Adams Miller

Haesun Moon

Kathryn Britton

Alejandra León De La Barra

Angela Koh

Tanya Cruz Teller

Marlene Ogawa

Thriving Women Thriving World

Cover and Design Layout: Deborah Stocco
Cover Art: Diana Whitney, reproduced with permission

Taos Institute Publications
A Division of the Taos Institute
Chagrin Falls, Ohio
USA

ISBN-13: 978-1-938552-68-7

TABLE OF CONTENTS

FOREWORD

by Mary Gergen

It is a great pleasure to write a foreword for this very special book. It comes into print 100 years after the passage of the 19th Amendment to the US Constitution. With that victory, women in my country were finally all allowed to vote. Women were finally considered full and equal citizens within the United States.

One hundred years later, women may be considered citizens, but how equal we are is still another matter. Women do not get equal pay for equal work. We are often discriminated against in promotions and selections to high-level jobs. We are often graded on a higher curve than our male peers. We tend to be victims of sexual assaults and harassments. The negative stereotypes about who we are remain strong. We live in the era of #MeToo, when women and men and others struggle to find common ground as an aura of conflict pervades our relationships.

Despite the plethora of scholarly and popular books, the hundreds of newspaper and magazine articles, and the endless media coverage, the way in which issues of women's concerns has been constructed has been highly reductive. All perspectives on gender issues tend to be negative, painted with a bitter brush. From exposés and critical assessments, to narratives of abuse, to the fomenting of action groups, the call has been to arms. Women and their supporters are asked to protest, to resist, and to fight against the patriarchal forces of oppression. The only way for feminists to approach this social dilemma is to respond aggressively.

This book is different. Here a new approach to feminist issues is being fomented. A spirit of optimism is being born. How exciting this is. In this volume, Diana Whitney and her coauthors seek to imagine a way forward that is not about creating adversaries, building barriers to understanding, finding ways to fight and defeat enemies, nor segregating ourselves in the process. It is another way, one that promises more in terms of female equality and more in terms of gender peace. It is not a laying down of arms, a compromise, nor a conciliatory posture that allows the continuation of male dominance. No, it is a new formulation that will enhance the lives of all people, regardless of how they identify as gendered beings and allow for the possibility that women can advance their goals without destroying men. It moves way beyond a battle of the sexes. Women and men, as well as those who refuse to be defined, can mutually gain what they want and do so on the same playing field.

This news is exciting indeed, but you might ask: How is this to be done? Diana Whitney has entered the field of feminist politics, appropriating the tools of her consultancy for issues related to gender troubles. Why should the struggles among/between the genders be any more difficult than those between corporate clients competing for the same outcomes? By invoking the knowledge and the principles of Appreciative Inquiry, she has found ways of opening entirely new doors to mutual understanding.

With her in this ambitious endeavor is a group of dedicated and smart feminists from diverse backgrounds and disciplines who understand that a way of forming new relational ties is through appreciative questions, not those that are hostile and oppositional. Within this book, approaches to change are highlighted that show more can be accomplished through appreciation than through aggression. Despite the traditions that emphasize power, solidarity, and willingness to resist opposition, something new may well yield more fruitful results. This is what each of the chapters provides.

This book is revolutionary. It occupies a new position in the firmament of feminist offerings; it constructs the world in ways that challenge all that has gone before. I think we will all benefit from the wisdom of the authors who, using Appreciative Inquiry, have created new possibilities for gender relationships, bringing us closer to the vision promised by the 19th amendment for true gender equality.

1

FROM #METOO TO THRIVING WOMEN

Introduction by Diana Whitney

This book is an invitation to journey from #MeToo to thriving women via inquiry, dialogue, and stories. It joins with thousands of other books, songs, paintings, protest marches, and performances that have emerged in response to the #MeToo movement. It addresses topics that may be difficult to talk about, yet must be talked about. To heal social wounds and create conditions that bring out the best of women worldwide, we need to talk and listen with compassion.

The state of women in the world today needs curiosity and communication, not any one set of answers. Answers close doors. They stop the flow of curiosity, compassion, and conversation. The purpose of this book is to open dialogue and storytelling that lead to relational healing and well-being. Questions open conversations, keep them going, and make listening interesting. They enhance mutual respect and collaboration. Stories illustrate uniquely personal experiences, life lessons for others to learn from and to embrace. This book is an invitation to dialogue, healing, and inspired actions.

If you are a consultant, facilitator, educator, coach, therapist, pastor, rabbi, imam, social worker, parent, friend, or lover wondering how to stimulate dialogue about gender issues with individuals, groups, or whole organizations, this book is for you. Throughout this book, you will find prompts and catalysts for conversations about issues affecting women.

THROUGH AN APPRECIATIVE LENS

Appreciative by choice, this book offers an antidote to the sexual abuse, injustice, and inequality we hear about, read about, and experience daily. We, the authors, are not without anger, frustration, and shame. We have suffered sexual harassment, date rape, verbal abuse, misogyny at home and at work, discrimination in churches, schools, health care, shopping, and work. We have seen our mothers, aunts, and grandmothers live without opportunities to fulfill their dreams. While we know suffering as women, we also know success in life as executives, consultants, coaches, mothers, wives, and friends. We have succeeded in a world in which men are favored and women often feel invisible. It has been extra work to fend off sexual jokes and harassment. It has been frustrating to be interrupted by men and to hear them make our ideas their own. Most significantly, it has been a challenge to adapt to male-favored practices at the expense of feminine ways of knowing and working. The state of the world for women is not as we wish it to be.

Our experience, however, shows that the best way to create social change is with *Appreciative Inquiry*, a practice that is life affirming, relationship enhancing, and world making. The Appreciative Inquiry process engages people in dialogue about their individual and collective strengths, their hopes and dreams for the future, and opportunities for collaborative actions.

The process generally follows an *Appreciative Inquiry 4-D Cycle,* which includes the following phases:

- Discovering the Best of the Past and Present
- Dreaming of Opportunities for the Future
- Designing Innovations for Positive Change
- Delivering Transformational Results

Appreciative Inquiry is both a philosophy and a methodology for positive change. It is founded on the assumption that we learn and grow in the direction of what we ask questions about, what we focus upon, and what we talk about regularly.

At the heart of Appreciative Inquiry are unconditionally positive questions that turn problems into a quest for positive possibilities. Appreciative Inquiry suggests that the questions we ask are fateful. They determine what we learn, and they influence how we go forward together.

Consider your answers to these two questions:

1. Who or what in life depletes your energy and depresses you?
2. Who or what energizes you and makes you want to do more?

These two questions are the flip sides of the same topic about your energy. Which question invites you to talk about what you want more of in your life? Which question inspires you to make things happen? Most people say that second question brings out their best, while the first is a downer! The more positive and uplifting our questions, the more energy we have for learning and positive action.

When we look at the world through an appreciative lens, we recognize that even though the world is not as we wish it were, there are instances of people, organizations, and communities that are creating thriving conditions for women and girls. There are places where the world works well for women. The purpose of Appreciative Inquiry questions is to help us discover these exemplary people, organizations, and communities, and then to learn from them. By doing so we generate potential for positive change. Appreciative Inquiry questions are invitations to seek and tell stories about positive possibilities, thereby shifting conversations from life's deficits to life-affirming potentials.

Consider, for example, the term *intersectionality*. Coined by Kimberlé Crenshaw, it represents an understanding that multiple forms of inequality or disadvantage sometimes compound themselves and create obstacles that often are not understood within conventional ways of thinking about social justice. We believe intersectionality to be a useful notion for helping disadvantaged women talk about and make sense of their lives and for bringing their unique needs to the attention of others.

We also wonder, however, how the term might serve as a meaningful metaphor for bringing out the best of women by exploring layers of strengths and wisdom developed by living with multiple forms of inequality or disadvantage. Without denying the burdens of intersectionality, an appreciative lens suggests that questions and conversations about strengths and wisdom garnered through intersectionality would enhance confidence and empowerment.

FROM #METOO TO THRIVING WOMEN

The origin of this book and its title came about when I began asking how Appreciative Inquiry might be used to make a positive difference in the lives of women and girls around the world. After the 2016 election in the United States, I began to feel angry. The more I heard stories of "pussy grabbing," "date rape," "#MeToo" and "#timeisup," the angrier I became. Talking with women friends and colleagues did nothing but fuel the fire. Everyone seemed to have another #MeToo story. It seemed epidemic. Talking about it drained my energy and put me on a downward emotional spiral. Wanting to pull myself up and out of the nosedive, I increased my meditation time, made daily gratitude lists, and wondered how I might reframe #MeToo into a life-affirming, action-inspiring topic.

I began my appreciative quest by wondering, "What is the flip side of #MeToo and everything it stands for?" For several months I asked myself, friends, and colleagues, "What do you want more of for women and girls in the world? What is your ideal world for women and girls?" As is often the case when applying Appreciative Inquiry, the first batch of answers emphatically described what we want less of: less sexual harassment and abuse, less coverup of abuse, less blaming the victims of rape, fewer barriers to education for girls and women, fewer white men making decisions about women's bodies, fewer women sabotaging each other. While passionate, these first responses did not offer guidance about what to do. Knowing what we want less of in our lives is very different from knowing what we want more of. Inspired actions follow the paths of our dreams, of how we want our world to be positively different.

As I kept asking, "What do we want more of?" the answers began to shift. We want more women in leadership, more attention to the needs of girls and women in schools, more male allies, more partnerships among women and men, more women entrepreneurs and business owners, more research by and about women, more inclusion, equal pay, and opportunities at work, more women supporting women, more fairness, equity, and safety. Taking these wishes together led to a major insight. What we want is for women worldwide to thrive, to be able to do and be whatever they choose to do and be. When women thrive, it benefits the world around them. The flip side of #MeToo became *Thriving Women, Thriving World*.

DOING LIFE TOGETHER

Nothing about #MeToo is singularly about women. #MeToo is a collective comment on the state of relationships in the world. In general, writings from the fields of psychology and personal growth focus on the individual and suggest that social change begins with individual change. Indeed, one contemporary mantra is "The only person you can change is yourself." This is one way of looking at the world. Another way is that we live and thrive in relationship. Consider misogyny. It is commonly thought of as an individual character trait of men who abuse women, as in, "He is a misogynist." In contrast, Kate Manne, in her groundbreaking book, *Down Girl, The Logic of Misogyny,* proposes misogyny as a dance between a woman who lives outside of socially accepted norms and a man who values the norms and feels a self-righteous justification to punish her. One definition locates misogyny as a quality of the man; the other definition locates it in the relationship. When relationships are caustic and abusive, women suffer. They have very different life options than when relationships are healthy and supportive.

Narratives surrounding women's status in the world are complex, affected by culture, community, and country, as well as by family, workplace, and religion. Consider the right to vote. While women have the legal right to vote in all countries today, it is not equally easy for them to exert that right. In some countries, a woman needs permission from her guardian, a husband, father, or older brother, to leave the house to vote. In other countries, the journey to vote is long and often dangerous. Legal rights do not guarantee free participation in society. Throughout this book, we invite explorations of what women can and cannot do and how they see themselves affected by the relationships, social norms, and power structures of their lives.

THRIVING = SUCCEEDING + DEVELOPING WELL

Thriving, as defined by the Cambridge online dictionary, is a way of being that encompasses both success and development. Thriving necessitates a blend of achievement and growth, accomplishment and learning, excellence and humility. It requires a balance of the demands for success with the demands for well-being and development.

Dr. Daniel Brown and colleagues at the University of Portsmouth, UK conducted a meta-review of research about thriving. Their findings are summarized by Ephrat Livni, "Thriving involves evolution whereas prospering only denotes success, especially financial. In other words, if you're just coasting, doing the unchallenging thing that you do well, you're not thriving because you're not developing. Similarly, if you're performing well and trying tough stuff but you're perpetually stressed and not enjoying yourself, that's success of a kind but doesn't count as thriving." Brown concludes that thriving occurs when success and development happen in tandem.

In her book, *Thrive,* Arianna Huffington declares "thrive" a third metric for success along with power and money, the two more traditional metrics. She describes the experience of thriving as a unique blend of success and well-being, a life imbued with wonder, wisdom, and giving.

Brown adds that thriving requires a number of external elements to line up. He suggests that no matter what one does, the experience of thriving depends on opportunities, connections with people, support, manageable challenges, a stable environment, and a high degree of autonomy. These are all topics explored in this book.

ABOUT THIS BOOK

The many conversations I had about #MeToo and its antidotes were provocative. They revealed a delicate desire among women and men to talk with each other about these issues in ways that are not blaming or harmful but instead strengthen relationships. From experience, I felt sure that a book of Appreciative Inquiry questions could open and guide affirmative conversations.

Determined to write such a book, I began gathering friends and colleagues with passion for women's issues, who were asking, "What can I do? How might Appreciative Inquiry help the cause?" Soon, a group of nine women ranging in age from 35 to 70, living in South Africa, Canada, Mexico, and the United States, and working on all seven continents had signed on as authors.

Recognizing that we could not possibly cover all the issues surrounding gender relations and the status of women in the world today, we chose topics that emerge from our own experiences. The result is 92 topics organized into ten chapters.

The questions on a given page are all related to the topic described at the top of that page. They begin by inviting you to Discover what is already strong and beneficial in your life. Subsequent questions ask you to Dream about ideal futures, to Design new ways of being, and to Deliver inspired actions.

While primarily a book of Appreciative Inquiry questions, there are a number of short stories woven throughout the book. Written by cherished colleagues, they are personal stories intended to awaken curiosity and prompt wondering about how you might support the many and diverse women in your life and work.

Throughout the book we use the pronouns "they" and "them" when referring to single individuals in order to use gender-neutral language.

In Chapter Two, we outline effective ways to use appreciative questions, including personal journaling, facilitating a thriving women's retreat, and changing organizational culture. In each case, we offer guidelines for you to follow or adapt to meet your needs.

In Chapters Three through Twelve, we provide an array of Appreciative Inquiry questions on topics related to thriving women. Each chapter is focused on an issue of significance: women thriving, body well-being, healing from relational abuse, education, financial savvy, work, women supporting women, men supporting women, thriving relationships, and living life as a work of art.

In Chapter Thirteen, we conclude by describing five practices for thriving, for being successful while developing well. We call them the arts of thriving.

This book is our gift to you. Share it, copy it, use it as it is, or adapt it and use it. Gather your friends and colleagues around the kitchen table, in the boardroom, or at the playground. Share stories, talk about what you can do together, and do it.

2
Ways to Use the Questions
in this Book

The topics in this book are not easily discussed. Indeed, they are often considered taboo or too sensitive for mixed company. Yet these conversations need to occur to heal, liberate, and bring out the best of women. We offer the following eight ways to use the questions in this book to help you have conversations, deepen understanding, and catalyze transformation on sensitive topics such as healing from abuse, making body choices, creating safe schools, asking for equal pay, and addressing exclusion at work.

To Inspire Journaling and Self Reflection

The questions in this book are excellent tools for personally reversing the tendency to spiral down the emotional tunnel of blame, shame, or depression. Each question is an invitation for you to reflect upon an important life issue using an appreciative lens.

Find a quiet place to sit with your journal and a favorite pen for 30 minutes to an hour. If you set a timer, set it for 5 minutes before your time is up so you have time to mindfully close your writing.

Scan this book and choose one topic question that is calling to you now. Think about why it is important to you. Read the question and sub questions out loud to yourself. Perhaps read them again. Take a few deep breaths. Now write your answers. Don't stop to think about what you are writing. Just write and write and write. After a while, write larger or smaller, or with your non-dominant hand. Write in prose or poetry, draw pictures, or scribble if you wish. Keep expressing your thoughts and feelings. Slowly reflect on your own answers, listening to your inner voices.

When you feel done writing, or when your alarm sounds, stop. Take a few deep breaths. End your journaling session by writing a short note of appreciation to yourself for the insights and wisdom revealed in your answers.

To Enliven an Important Relationship

You have a friend, a colleague, or maybe an intimate partner who just doesn't get it. You value each other, and yet you wonder how to talk about hot topics such as sexual abuse, unfair pay for women, or boosting women into leadership. The questions in this book can prompt meaningful conversations and deepen trusting relationships.

Choose one topic and set of questions from the book to serve as the focus for your conversation. Invite your friend or colleague to have a conversation with you. Explain why it is important to you. Share that your hope is to learn together and strengthen your already good relationship. Ask your partner for an hour or more. Face-to-face is preferable, but online conversations can also be meaningful.

When you meet, begin by thanking your partner for joining you for this conversation. Share your vulnerability about the topic and the conversation. Give your partner a copy of this book, opened to the topic and questions that you have selected. Explain that you want to have a mutually appreciative interview followed by a discussion about what you learn. Explain that you will take turns interviewing for 20 minutes each, using the same questions. Agree that whatever you share will remain between the two of you.

Interview your partner for 20 minutes, then take a stretch break and swap roles. After both of the interviews are complete, discuss the following questions:

- What did you learn about each other from the stories, thoughts, and feelings shared?
- What surprised you about yourself as you shared your stories, thoughts, and feelings?

- How have the interviews and discussion enlivened and strengthened your relationship?

Pause and take a couple of deep breaths together. Say thank you, and share one or two things you cherish about your relationship.

TO FACILITATE A THRIVING WOMEN RETREAT

You want to host a retreat to enhance awareness and inspire actions on behalf of women and girls in your community. Your first decision is who should be there. Do you want to host an all-women's retreat, or do you want to foster dialogue among women and men? Both are worthwhile, but they will be different.

Once you have issued the invitations, it's time to design your retreat. We suggest you follow an Appreciative Inquiry 4 D process:

Discovery – Select one or two topics and questions to discover participants' strengths and successes. Conduct one-on-one interviews followed by a discussion about surprises and inspirations.

Dream – Select a topic and questions to foster imagination and future thinking. Invite participants in small groups to creatively express – in drawings, poetry, or skits – their dreams for a thriving world, for women in their communities, and for themselves.

Design – Select a topic and questions to stimulate conversation about specific changes that are needed for participants to realize their dreams. Discuss what can be done personally and collectively.

Destiny – As the retreat draws to an end, discuss individual plans and commitments, collective actions for change, and how the group will stay connected and support each other going forward.

As part of your closing comments or ritual, consider giving copies of *Thriving Women, Thriving World* to all the participants. Ask them to share the book and their experiences at the retreat with others. Invite them to share their commitment, what they will do to support thriving women in their communities and workplaces.

To Create Ripples of Conversation

You may wish that your friends, family, church groups, or colleagues were more sensitive to women's issues. You'd like to have one big conversation and include them all. One way to this is by creating ripples of conversation: you talk with a few people, ask them to talk with a few more people, and so forth until somebody says we should all get together and talk about this!

To start the wave, select one topic and questions from the book and approach three to five people. The more people, the more ripples. Start the conversation as an interview. As you interview people, they may feel curious and ask to hear your answers to the same questions. When this happens give them a copy of the questions and invite them to approach other people. Suggest that they keep the ripple going, and cycle back to let you know about the most exciting, powerful, or revealing conversation they've had.

Our experience suggests that at some point you will begin hearing about the impact of the ripple of conversation you started. People will share how the conversations changed the way they see things or what they do. You will hear stories of people who got the book and started a ripple of conversation in another organization or community. These conversations are meaningful. They change lives, organizations, and the world. Have fun keeping the ripples going.

To Catalyze a Thriving Culture at Work

While many organizations around the world – corporations, hospitals, government agencies, and schools – espouse a commitment to inclusion, they often find it challenging to put the commitment into practice. Are you wondering how your organization might enhance gender equality, safety, and inclusion?

The questions in this book can be used to move a team or a whole organization to inspired actions. Start by inviting a small, diverse group of people from across the organization to join you. They may be part of the same department, or they may span different functions, levels, or locations. Give each person a copy of the book, and invite them each to identify one or two topics and questions that reflect what they want more of in the organization.

Gather the group. Have people introduce themselves and share the topics and questions they've selected, including *why* they chose them. Then together, with a focus on what you want to grow within your organization, select three topics and questions to create a *Thriving Women, Thriving World* interview guide. Begin your interview guide with a new question that asks people to introduce themselves. Close it with a new question that invites them to imagine the organization's best future full of thriving women. Decide how many interviews each of you will do and with whom. Schedule and conduct interviews. Have people take notes of all the great stories and ideas they hear.

After you have finished conducting interviews, reconvene the group to share what you learned. Summarize your findings into these categories:

- What we are already doing well to support women
- What people hope and dream for our future
- Specific actions we can take to enliven our organization as a great place for thriving women to work

Share your findings with all the people you interviewed, your supervisors, and your colleagues. Ask them what they find most surprising and what they might do to make a positive difference. Suggest that they conduct interviews and hold similar conversations with others to further catalyze awareness and inspired actions across the organization.

Bring your original group together a few months later. Share stories about positive changes you have experienced. Celebrate the new ways your organization brings out the best of women.

To Enhance Intergenerational Story Telling

You may be an elder wanting to share your experiences with younger women and girls in your family or at work. You may be a younger woman wishing you could hear stories and learn from the successful women around you. Using the questions in this book for intergenerational storytelling may give you just what you want.

First decide if you want to have one-on-one conversations or gather a small group. Then review the topics and questions in this book and choose two or three that interest you and that you are curious to understand from other people's points of view.

Next invite people to talk with you. If you are doing this as a one-on-one conversation, consider a comfortable and safe space for your chat. It may be a conference room visit, a conversation over a meal or cup of coffee, or a walk together. Be sure to explain what you want to talk about and how long you imagine it will take.

If you are hosting a group storytelling session, be sure to find a space that will feel welcoming and safe for everyone. Consider providing snacks since the conversation could last as long as two hours. Let everyone know who else you've invited and what you wish to discuss together.

In preparation for either approach, we suggest that you read over the questions that you have chosen and if necessary, rewrite them in your own words. This will make it easier for you to ask them and set a storytelling tone. You may even want to answer the questions yourself to see how your answers flow. Remember your goal is to foster heart-felt storytelling and intergenerational learning.

Intergenerational storytelling can uncover surprising memories and emotions. For those who share their stories, it is a gift to be asked and know that others want to learn from them. For listeners, it is gift to receive another person's wise legacy.

To Change Problem Talk into Possibility Talk

Are you tired of hearing your friends and family members talk about gender inequality and abuse without doing anything about it? Is your daily news a never-ending stream of problems? Do you find yourself getting frustrated and wondering what you could do about a specific issue affecting the lives of women and girls?

Fret no more. You can use the questions in this book to change *problem talk into possibility talk*. You can use them to stimulate positive change about a problem in your organization or community.

Begin by articulating your problem or frustration. Then review the many topics and questions in this book until you find one or two that affirmatively address your specific frustration. Appreciative questions can turn your frustration into a quest for positive possibilities.

Once you have your appreciative questions, gather an informal group of people from different areas of the organization or community who share your interest in the issue. Consider inviting people who have resources, information, and funds to contribute. Invite those who will be affected by any changes that might occur. Invite people who are the loudest voices for maintaining the current situation.

Bring everyone together. Explain that you want their help to shift problem talk to possibility talk and to create positive change. Use the topics and questions you have selected as a basis for dialogue. As people share and discuss answers to the questions, they will learn each other's points of view and build shared commitment to collaborative actions. By engaging people in possibility talk, you build compassion and momentum for collaboration and positive change. It is amazing how much people commit to what they help create with possibility talk.

To Conduct Research for Social Change

While research by women and about women is on a steady rise, much more research is needed to understand both the lived experiences of women and girls and their unique needs for education, health care, and leadership development. The questions in this book provide provocative ideas for conducting this research.

Appreciative Inquiry questions are affirmative, relational, and world-making by design. They are aimed at enhancing knowledge about what contributes to success, growth, and thriving. Research conducted using Appreciative Inquiry stimulates social change because it explores what works rather than what does not. By engaging people whose lives and futures are at stake, this form of research simultaneously creates change and catalyzes learning and knowledge building. Social change happens in the process of sharing and collecting stories. When women interview women, they benefit in two ways. As they are being interviewed, they experience being the experts of their own lives, often for the first time. As they interview and hear stories of other women who faced the same or similar challenges and thrived, they learn new ways of going forward.

The questions in this book can serve as a basis for action research in organizations and communities. They can be combined into an interview guide to collect stories and stimulate learning for hundreds, even thousands of women, girls, and male allies around the world. A wealth of knowledge and social transformation awaits discovery using the questions in this book.

3
THRIVING WOMEN AT THEIR BEST

When you hear the words, "thriving woman," who comes to mind?
Where is she? What does she say and do that leads you to see her
as thriving? Who is with her? What are they talking about and
doing? What is it like for you to see her, know her, and be with her?

If we were to collect all of our answers to these questions, it would
be evident that thriving women come in all body sizes and shapes,
with all colors and tongues, with or without formal education, with
or without paid work. Thriving women are found in every fold of
our socioeconomic strata. Our answers would describe places where
women feel safe to gather, work, and celebrate, places where they
freely express themselves, and places where they feel welcomed and
included as equal yet gloriously different.

Our stories would be rich with emotions, expressions, and
achievements moving in, out, and between the lives of these women
and the people with them. We would tell of relational wealth, families educating girls to lead the world, friendships sustaining women
through sadness and joy, women and male allies supporting women
and inspiring them to be their best. We would talk of the collaboration that occurs when women are treated as valued equal partners.

Our answers would reflect the pattern-breaking, trouble-making,
and social-norm-changing ways of thriving women. We would
describe them as curious, learning, and getting results that contribute to their families, communities, and a sustainable world.

Sharing stories of thriving women would energize us, just as we
have been in their presence. Telling their stories would delight us
and remind us of their guidance, leadership, and love. We would
feel grateful to know such women and to have experienced such
moments with them.

These moments that energize, embody, and uplift our individual and collective best selves are what we call *thriving*. All people who identify as women whether by nature or by choice, and those they love and are loved by are invited to the journey of thriving.

Thriving is something we do along with those who see the best of us, who nudge us to pioneer new possibilities, and who join us to celebrate the steps we've taken to keep on keeping on. Thriving invites each of us to stretch beyond individual endeavors toward relational symbiosis defined by coordinated attention, conversation, and movement together.

Thriving women are extraordinary ordinary women. They are mothers and daughters, teachers and hairdressers, nurses and doctors, scientists and sales reps, girls and elders. In other words, they lead ordinary lives in extraordinary ways. Their secret ingredient is unwavering dedication to gender equality, self-sovereignty, and creating conditions for other women and girls, now and in the future, to live free and fulfilling lives. Thriving women are part of the long arc of evolution moving our world toward joyful freedom for all.

The questions, stories, and practices in this chapter invite you to join with others to share stories and explore ideals in support of thriving women at their best.

If the three wise men had been women, they would have asked directions, arrived on time, helped deliver the baby, cleaned the stable, made a casserole, brought practical gifts, and there would be Peace on Earth.

Dee Dee Myers

3-1. THRIVING WOMEN AT OUR BEST

Some women make a habit of thriving. They live on the upside of life, achieving their goals while having enough time and energy to hug the whole world. They move through their days with balance and mindfulness. They accomplish what they set out to do, while catching the joy and juiciness of life.

1. Tell me about a time you experienced thriving, a time you achieved a goal and had energy to spare. What was the situation?

   » Who else was involved? How did they contribute to your experience of thriving?

   » What did you do that made this a time of thriving?

   » How did you feel at this time?

2. Tell me about a time you took on a challenge that put you on a steep learning curve and you met the challenge gloriously. What was the situation?

   » How did you learn what you needed in order to succeed?

   » Who and what was most helpful to you in this situation?

   » What can others learn from this experience about thriving through challenges?

3. Tell me about women who come to your mind when you hear the words thriving women. Who are they?

   » How do you feel when you are with them?

   » What would you like to ask them or learn from them?

   » Who or what supports them to be thriving women?

3-2. RELATIONAL SAVVY

Most women experience themselves as skilled caretakers, purveyors of relational savvy in service to their families, friends, teams, and communities. For some women it comes easily. Others feel burdened and wish someone would help or care for them in return. It feels good and is uplifting when our relational savvy is seen and celebrated. That includes all the ways that we care, serve, help, and support.

1. If I were to ask three or four of your friends, family, or colleagues to describe your relational savvy, what would they say?

   » How would they describe you at your best when you are caring, supporting, and helping?

   » What about these descriptions most resonates with your own sense of self?

   » What are you be most proud to hear?

2. Describe a time when your relational savvy saved the day.

   » What did you do or say that contributed to this success?

   » How did you involve and inspire others?

   » How did you keep everyone on the same page?

   » How did you celebrate small successes along the way?

3. Tell me about a time when you made the choice to say "Not my job to care for another," and it was the right decision.

   » What was the situation?

   » How did you do it? What did you do or say?

   » How did your relational savvy help you take care of yourself in this situation?

Dark Water Runs Deep

A Message to My White Women Friends via My Mother's Wisdom

by Rita Anita Linger, Ph.D.

There is so much texture and complexity to those of us who are women and of darker skin. While we smile when we want to cry, and we are often in awe of racial hatred and its origins, these experiences enable us to see the root causes of life's issues; if we open ourselves to a place of vulnerability, we become fearless, balanced, and a conduit of hope, strength, and resilience.

As a woman of color raised by women of Antiguan and Dominican ethnicity, growing up in the lower east side of Manhattan, I learned as soon as I emerged from my mother's womb that I was a citizen of the world. This was the designation for all who were born in my community of such deep diversity, no matter what ethnicity or hue. I was also taught that I was powerful. My mother instilled in me early on that I had to do my best in everything had to work harder than my white counterparts to experience similarly successful results because they were born into a world of privilege, perhaps not socio-economically, but as a result of the color of their skin, a "gift" provided at inception.

"Dark water runs deep," my mother used to say, "and because of your ancestral history of suffering and oppression, your spirit understands the value of responding to difficulty over reacting to it. That will be your saving grace." My mother paid very specific attention to gender issues and differences in the US. She ingrained in me an understanding that the only glass ceilings that existed were in my mind. She used to say, "It is how you see yourself that will guide your ability to navigate relationships with men."

Another of her truths to me was, "Do not compromise your values, and know without a doubt that your gender does not preclude you from doing or accomplishing anything you can envision. Don't be ashamed to confront sexism or abuse of any kind. All women are Goddesses. Some of them just don't know it."

My mother, who was an artist, model, and fashion designer for some of Hollywood's elite like Tyrone Powers, told me to confront things that are uncomfortable, particularly those that involved male/female interactions. "If a man looks at you inappropriately, if he touches you in a way that makes you feel uncomfortable, don't wait. Confront the situation immediately. Your persona, your self-respect demands that of you." Her advice helped me through several experiences of sexual harassment in the corporate workplace. When I was looked at or had comments directed to me in a way that was not appropriate, I would say, with confidence, a sense of boldness and with respect imbued with my mother and grandmother's strength, "Excuse me. Don't look at me like that. It's not appropriate, and I don't like it. So, just stop it. I'll only tell you once, and then if it happens again, we've got a problem." It worked, and in each of those experiences, I felt empowered and not at all anxious. I knew that the spirit of my ancestors was holding me with boldness.

So, my white sisters, while women of color have as our legacy a history of oppression, slavery, genocide, and trauma, we have had sage teachers in our homes and families. We've learned how to sit with discomfort, especially sexism and sexual assault, topics that are present but hidden from view in the lives of many women of color. Know that we might be able to offer you sage advice. Know that we are sure to lift you up and help you recognize your power. Know that our DNA is only one point off from yours. Know that together, we can support each other in ways we cannot do on our own. Reach out to us in your time of need and despair. We are here for you, now and always. You and I are powerful, strong. We are survivors, and we are more alike than not. Dark water runs deep, and those waters are here to buoy you through your darkest times. Because my mother and grandmother understood the power of the woman.

3-3. INHERITED NARRATIVES

Inherited narratives tell us what people, culture, and community expect of us in order to fit in, belong, and succeed. They are messages we receive from parents, grandparents, teachers, and other significant authority figures. Most of the time, we make life decisions guided by these inherited narratives. There are times, however, when we need to challenge them and break patterns and social norms that keep us from being our best.

1. Tell me a story from your childhood that shaped you. What was the situation? When did it happen?

   » Why has this story been meaningful to you?

   » How has it influenced the way you relate with others?

   » How has the way you tell this story changed over time?

2. Think about all the stories that you tell about yourself.

   » What two or three stories about yourself do you repeat when you meet new people?

   » Why do these stories matter to you?

3. Describe a time when you outgrew an inherited narrative, when you consciously decided to be different or to do something different. What was the situation?

   » What was the inherited narrative that no longer served you?

   » What new story did you create?

   » What did you do differently to create a new self-story?

   » How did it feel to let go of the old narrative?

4. Imagine, someone is telling a story inspired by you, about something important they learned from you or about something amazing you did. What would the story be about?

MAKING DREAMS MATTER

by Haesun Moon

"Mommy, guess what happened in my dream last night," was often my opening line for the day as I awoke as a four-year-old. "Tell me what happened," she would say as she reclined on my tiny bed and I scooted my tiny body over to make room for her. "So, here's what happened." I would tell her everything I remember from my dream, some parts already becoming hazy. "And then?" she would nudge me as she listened, making curious noises, "Mhm" and "Ah." By the time my dream story took several "And then" turns, my story was clearer than my dream.

"Well, that really is a good dream. You know why?" she'd add after every dream. Flying meant I was getting taller, picking flowers meant good news was on its way, and teeth falling out meant resolved problems (whatever the problems may be for a four-year-old). Then one day I had a dream of tripping down the stairs. When she responded in her usual way, I challenged her. "But Mommy, how can this be a good dream? Didn't you say last time that climbing the stairs was a good dream? This is the opposite of that." "Well..." she said with her eyebrows slightly raised and a smile. "Look closely. It's a different staircase, my love." Mommy made every dream matter, and there was always another way to look at it.

Several decades later as I sit with my coaching clients, I am often reminded of this cherished memory of my childhood. People bring lots of "So, here's what happened," stories. Some seem readier to tell their stories than others. Some stories sound more rehearsed than others. As they narrate, I sit saying "Mhm," and "Ah," with every turn they make in their stories. I am curious not only about what happened, but more about how they want their stories to end. I ask, "Suppose, just suppose... somehow this story ends in the way that makes your heart sing.

What might you notice that's even better than it has been?" I get to see my clients sit with the new stories they are invited to tell.

Their stories now take a detour from their familiar routes. As I nudge with occasional "And then what happens?" I get a tour of their hopes and dreams that gives me a glimpse of what they truly care about. Now they tell a story of what matters instead of what's the matter in their lives. They are curating their hopes and dreams.

My hope is for you to curate, not narrate, your stories. The word, curate, comes from its Latin root "cura" meaning care. Indeed, the act of selecting, organizing, and presenting the stories we care about is an active choice of taking care of ourselves and others. No wonder the same root is shared with the word cure since this can be a healing experience from being inflicted with unwelcome stories.

Curiosity is another word that bears the word cura at its heart. As a conversation partner, what you are curious about will orient the other's attention. If you are curious about what's the matter, you set them on a path with your questions to look closely into what's wrong, what's not working, and what might be getting in their way. If you are curious about what matters to them, you are inviting them to be on a quest to discover what truly matters and what makes their hearts sing. That is a choice we can make, a new way of telling and hearing stories.

3-4. The Root Cause of Our Awesomeness

We are all exceptional and awesome in our own ways. No one is exactly like you or me. We all have a unique array of values, beliefs, personality quirks, and ways of being. We could say, that taken together, this describes the root cause of our awesomeness!

1. Putting modesty aside, tell me about some of the values and beliefs that make you unique. Why are you proud of them?
    »   When did you first notice these qualities about yourself?
    »   Did you recognize them, or did someone point them out?
    »   Where did they come from?
    »   When do they show up in your life most clearly?

2. Tell me about a time when you were able to do something that no one else could do. What was the situation?
    »   What did you do?
    »   How did your uniqueness help?
    »   What did you learn about trusting your own ways of being?

3. Tell me about a time when your values or beliefs compelled you to go against the grain and make an unpopular decision. What did you say or do?
    »   Why did you feel compelled to go against the grain?
    »   What happened as a result?

4. Imagine receiving an award that reflects your uniqueness. What would the award be called?
    »   What would the person giving the award say about you?
    »   Why is this meaningful to you?
    »   How does receiving this award make you feel?

⮎ A Practice: An Appreciative Shower

by Amanda Trosten-Bloom

This practice is a simple and powerful way to saturate someone who we respect and care for with *gratitude* for all they've given. By allowing them to know their impact, this practice can change the way people see and understand themselves.

An Appreciative Shower can come in the form of a proclamation, a certificate of appreciation, a treasure chest, or a gift box filled with positive memories, wishes, and more. Consider the following as you plan an appreciative shower for (name of the person).

Identify contributors. Are you celebrating a birthday? Anniversary? Accomplishment? Life transition? Find people with insight into both the woman and the milestone to invite to participate.

Send prompting questions, and ask people to respond in writing. The questions might be as simple as:

» What strengths, gifts, and talents has (name) brought to you, this organization/community, and the world?

» Share a picture or story that captures a high point in your relationship with (name).

» What are your hopes and dreams for (name) in the years ahead?

Collect and assemble responses. Package them nicely. If possible, leave people's *personal* contributions in as raw a form as possible: handwritten, photographs, signatures, and so on. The relationships that are reflected therein are part of the gift.

Present it ceremoniously! If possible, present it in community. Again, this is a gift of *connection* made more meaningful when those who have co-created it are part of the giving.

3-5. Small Decisions Matter

Life emerges from the many small decisions we make: decisions to talk with someone or not, decisions to yell or be quiet, decisions to stay or leave. Small decisions can be surprisingly significant. Consider the person who notices a strange man who seems lost. They decide to ask if he needs directions. He decides not to end his life because someone cared enough to talk with him. Or, the person who walks into a class by mistake, decides to stay and discovers the subject that becomes their life work. Small decisions matter.

1. Tell me about a seemingly small decision you've made that led to significant and positive results. What was the decision?

    »   How did you make this decision?

    »   Who else was involved? What did they do?

    »   How has this decision become significant in your life?

2. Tell me about a turning point in your life that positively influenced your growth. What was the situation?

    »   What are some of the decisions that you made at the time?

    »   How did these decisions positively affect the outcome?

3. Imagine, a woman tells you that she is at a decision point in her life. She asks for guidance. What story would you tell to help her understand that small decisions can have great significance?

4. Think of a small decision you are facing now. Knowing what you know about the potential impact of small decisions, what do you think you will do?

A Letter to a Young Friend

by Marian Franson Scott

Laura, you can't imagine how flattering it is for me to be invited by someone of a younger generation to reminisce.

It was wartime throughout my college career. Pearl Harbor was attacked my freshman year, Hiroshima was bombed during my honeymoon in 1945, just after I graduated. Besides the fact that women's liberation was just beginning to take form, the chaos of wartime cultivated a lemming-like move to the altar: we all wanted to get married, have children, have homes. I had had the dream of becoming a journalist, but I quickly traded that ambition for the security of marrying Bill when he returned from the European front.

I did well in graduate school and was given a scholarship to continue, but I didn't seriously consider becoming a professional. I felt my role was as a supporting, not competing, wife. When Bill received a Fulbright Scholarship for a year in Paris, I was blissfully happy with the choices I had made. We had a wonderful year, traveling the Continent, visiting your grandparents several times in Oxford. I came home pregnant.

The landscape where you stand, at the brink of your adult life, is so very different from mine. Women have been liberated, not just the exceptional ones, but across the board. The choices and opportunities may be overwhelming, but at least you aren't limited. A few years of free fall are probably not a bad idea – just savoring life in your own way (as I would describe my early years of marriage in New Haven and Paris). Jumping from college into career or into marriage-with-children might prove too confining, even a mistake as you look backwards, as I am doing here, from your eighth decade. These are your luxury years when you can keep sensitive and searching for what your inner self really is trying to tell you. Pause and smell the roses. But don't become passive and let the years roll over you. Make choices. Take a few risks. Love, Marian

3-6. Caring Enough to Confront

At its best, confronting is an act of caring. While confronting is often seen as the opposite of caring, we have all confronted someone or something because we cared enough and believed things could be better. It may have been an impasse with someone over work, money, or attention. Whatever the situation, caring enough to confront made a positive difference.

1. Tell me about a time when someone cared enough to confront you and talk with you about something. What was the situation?

   » How did they approach you? What did they say?

   » How did they express care as they confronted you?

   » How did you respond at the time? How did you feel?

   » How did the conversation improve your relationship?

2. Now tell me about a time when you cared enough to confront and it made a positive difference. What was the situation?

   » What did you do and say?

   » How did the other person respond?

   » What did you learn from this situation that can help others confront injustice, harassment, or gender inequality?

3. Imagine that you are invited to teach a group of teenage girls how to care enough to confront. What would you tell them?

   » How would you help them clarify what they care about?

   » What would you teach as the three most important abilities for caring enough to confront?

   » How would you help them practice these abilities?

3-7. Challenging Gender Injustice

Every day, women face gender-based injustices that show up in subtle and not so subtle ways. Consider, for example, pink razors with higher price tags than the blue ones sitting beside them on the store shelf. Consider a woman having her paid lesson with a trainer interrupted by a man seeking information about the gym equipment. The question is not, "Do these subtle injustices exist?" They do. The question is, "How do we handle gender-based injustices?"

1. Tell me about a time when you effectively challenged gender injustice at work, at home, or in your community. What was the situation?

   » What did you do?

   » Why was it important for you to do this?

   » What pushback did you get from other people? How did you handle it?

   » What differences has your challenge to this injustice made for you and for others?

   » What lessons do you take from this experience?

2. Now, if you encounter an injustice in the future, how might you handle it differently to be more effective?

   » What would you say or do to make your point clear?

   » Who would you involve as allies?

3. Imagine, one big dream, a world free of gender injustice. Describe this new world to me. What wrongs would be set right?

   » What would be different at home? At work? In your community? In the whole world?

   » How would the world be better for girls? For women?

3-8. Designing Conditions for Thriving

Thriving happens in part by chance, in part by choice, and in part by conditions that bring out the best of people. Leadership, laws, access to resources, compelling purpose, creative colleagues, and safe spaces all play a part in generating a fertile milieu for thriving.

1. Think about the places where you spend your time at work or in leisure. Tell me about one place that is especially designed to support thriving. What is special about it?

   » What about the place is welcoming to people?

   » What about it supports thriving?

   » What about it would you like to see in other places?

2. Tell me about a time when you were at your thriving best. What conditions fostered your thriving?

   » How did you get involved?

   » Who else was there? How did you interact with them?

   » What did leadership and collaboration look like?

   » How did resources such as time, money, and materials help?

   » What rules, regulations, or norms were helpful?

3. Describe an exemplary organization with optimal conditions for thriving. What makes it exemplary?

   » Who are the participants of this organization?

   » What distinguishes them?

   » How are they supported to be their thriving best selves?

   » How is the organization designed so that thriving is inevitable?

☕ A Practice: Imagine Your Thriving Future

This activity is an opportunity to imagine and create a vision for your thriving future. As you envision your preferred future, you will also mobilize your mind, body, and soul toward thriving now.

This practice can be done alone or with a partner. If you do it alone, write down your answers to the questions. If you do it with a partner, ask your partner to record your answers as they listen.

First, close your eyes, activate your imagination, and see yourself waking up tomorrow as your best self.

- » What do you see and hear as you wake up?
- » Where are you? What are you doing? With whom?
- » What is energizing you? Inspiring you?

Second, imagine and see a day in the life of your thriving self.

- » What are you doing? What else?
- » Who are you with? What you saying to them?
- » How is being your thriving self positively affecting your relationships?

Third, imagine this thriving day coming to an end.

- » What are you doing to end your day well?
- » What have you learned during this thriving day?
- » For whom and what are you grateful?
- » What will you continue on the next day and beyond?

Fourth, open your eyes. What changes will you make in your life now to come closer to your imagined thriving future?

GIDDY UP GORGEOUS

by Lizanne Corbit

Inner Beauty owned
Outer Beauty dismissed

Betrayal of my Adorable
Betrayal of my Splendor

Dismissed Beauty
Disowned Beauty
Disavowed Beauty

Turn over the Soul Soil
For your Forgotten Beauty
Sift and Lift
Your Beauty Up
Honor Love
Nurture Cherish

Love your Splendor
God's Given Gift
Of Beauty

Remember the Freedom
Of being unburdened
Beauty!
Beauty up sister!
Saddle up and put on your spurs
It's going to be a Glorious ride!

Giddy up
Gorgeous
Mmwa and kisses
And Yahoo!

Yippee Kayo Ki Yah!
And Goddess Bless

4
CLAIMING OWNERSHIP OF OUR BODIES

Women are the owners of their bodies and the authors of their lives.

When it comes to freedom from control and ownership of our bodies, we see progress, and yet we must yell, "Not enough!" Women across the world trace their lineages back to women who were not free, who were property, either as wives, concubines, prostitutes, or slaves. Even today, in parts of the world, women live as property, owned and controlled by men. The struggle for freedom is a physical one. It abides in our relationships with our bodies as much as it resides in our thoughts, our language, our daily routines, and most certainly in the social norms governing our relationships. In her book, *Sacred Pleasure,* Riane Eisler states,

> "Today, at least in principle, the ownership of one person's body by another…and the negation of a person's right to make fundamental life choices is almost universally condemned. But there is one area where, even in principle, all this has been particularly resistant to change. When it comes to women's bodies…and choices, the traditional notion that men should hold power, make choices and control women's bodies is still ideologically, legally and economically in place throughout much of our world today."

Claiming ownership of our bodies means making our own choices about how we look and dress, whom we love and how we love them, whether we have children and with whom. It means creating safety at home, in our communities, at school, in our churches, on the streets, and at work. In all places where men of power act entitled to our bodies, we are taking back our bodies.

We recognize that the view of women as property lingers strongly in relationships among women and men today. We challenge relational norms that grant men the right to regulate the way women and girls dress and appear in society, that give men the power to use and abuse women and girls verbally, emotionally, and sexually, and that enable men to prohibit women's free expression and safe movement. We claim ownership of our bodies, our sexual orientations, and our body choices.

We know that as we change, so must our relationships. Relationships, families, and societies change in coordinated movement much like a rubber band. A pull in one direction creates tension in another. Our lives change as we articulate our choices, preferences, and orientations, challenge stereotypes, and reveal stories of abuse. We understand that our choices and changes may disrupt the lives of the people around us, their ways of making meaning, their balance of relationships, and their self-identities.

For all too long, women have been excluded from conversations, debate, and decision-making about their bodies and their lives. Decisions were made for them, not by them. We are committed to doing it differently, to including you – the women, men, and children we love – in dialogue, discernment, and decision-making about our bodies and our life choices. In return we ask that you seek to understand our hopes and dreams, accept our life choices, and support our self-sovereignty.

The questions, stories, and practices in this chapter are prompts for meaningful relationship-enhancing conversations to share your stories, challenge social norms, and claim ownership of your body.

Q: What's special about your vagina?

A: Somewhere deep inside it, I know it has a really smart brain.

Eve Ensler

4-1. Learning to Love Our Bodies

Learning to love our bodies is a lifelong endeavour. For some, it may require healing from verbal or sexual violations that occurred at an early age. For others it may be a daily challenge to avoid the bombardment of images and messages about the ideal body that we don't have. For all of us it means making peace with the ever-changing nature of our bodies going through puberty, becoming sexual, childbearing, menopause, and aging.

1. Let's start with a positive body scan. Tell me three things that you really like about your body. They might include how you move or what you look like. What are your three things?

2. Recall a body-affirming learning experience, a time when you learned something about your body that has helped you care for yourself and your body over the years. What did you learn?

   » How did you learn this?

   » How has this helped you over the years?

3. Do you remember how you learned about menstruation? Tell me the story.

   » How did you feel at the time?

   » How did the way you learned and the language used influence your feelings about your body?

4. What body issues are you facing now?

   » How are you learning what you need to know at this time?

   » Who are your best teachers? Companions on the journey?

   » What do they do or say that helps you learn about and love your body?

4-2. Smiling in the Mirror

For many of us, our *self-esteem*, how we feel about ourselves, and our appearance, are closely connected. Feeling attractive, pretty, or beautiful boosts our self-esteem making us ready to take on the world. It works both ways. Positive self-esteem from being our best and achieving our goals makes us smile in the mirror!

1. Tell me about a time when you smiled in the mirror. What was it that made you smile?

    » What gave you the sense of beauty at this time?

    » What made you feel good about yourself?

    » How did feeling beautiful affect your actions?

2. It energizes women to be recognized as beautiful and brilliant, attractive and able to accomplish great things. Recall a time when you felt all these things. What was the situation?

    » What contributed to you feeling brilliant and beautiful?

    » Who else was involved? What did they say or do?

3. Tell me about an older woman who is brilliant and beautiful. What about her is beautiful to you?

    » How is she brilliant?

    » How do you show her that you appreciate her beauty?

4. Imagine a world where girls and women of all body types, colors, and ages are smiling in the mirror and where they are honored as beautiful and brilliant. What would be different?

    » What would be making them smile in the mirror?

    » What would people be saying and doing?

4-3. Keeping Ourselves Safe

As much as we wish it were not so, the world can be dangerous for everyone, especially for women and children. People prepare to protect themselves in advance of snowstorms, hurricanes, or monsoons. Women also do things to keep themselves safe from physical or sexual harm so that they can care for themselves, should the need arise.

1. Tell me about a time when you felt safe and secure in your body. Was it a moment, a phase of your life, or your way of life?
    » Who or what helped make this possible for you?
    » What do you do to maintain your sense of safety?

2. Imagine you are getting ready to go out by yourself at night to an unfamiliar place. What will you do to ensure your safety?
    » Do you have a personal list of things you do whenever you leave the house? What actions are on the list?
    » How did you learn to do these things?
    » Who told you or showed you?
    » Something happens that makes you feel unsafe. What do you do to regain your sense of safety?

3. Recall a time when another woman gave you helpful tips for taking care of yourself in a new environment. You might have been traveling, starting a new job, looking for a new home, or setting out on a solo hike. What was the situation?
    » Who was she? What was your relationship?
    » What advice did she give you?
    » How did this advice help you keep yourself safe?

4. Think of the younger woman and girls who are important to you. What advice do you have about how to keep themselves safe?

4-4. CONSENT – TOUCHING HER ON HER TERMS

Consent is a healthy boundary that keeps girls and women safe. A violation of consent is a violation of a woman. Recently, women of all ages have come forward to share #MeToo stories of men who did not ask, did not take no for an answer, or used their power to impose sexually. The courage of these women and their stories, point to the need for consent, touching on her terms, as a social norm to protect women's physical, sexual, and emotional safety.

1. Tell me about your comfort with touching.

    »   When is it okay for people to touch you without asking?

    »   When do they need to ask for your consent?

2. Recall a #MeToo story that you've heard or read.

    »   What did it feel like to hear or read this story?

    »   How was consent violated?

    »   What does this story teach about the importance of consent?

3. Share a story about a time when you said no and were respected for doing so. What was the situation?

    »   Why did you say no?

    »   How did you indicate that you really meant no?

    »   How did that make you feel?

    »   How did you learn to expect consent?

4. Imagine you are invited to speak to a group of Boy Scouts about consent, what it looks like, and why it is important. What would you say?

4-5. Removing Her from Harm's Way

There are times when a girl or a woman needs help getting out of harm's way. She may have gone out for the night and had too much to drink. She may live in a verbally or physically violent family. She may be an abused spouse without resources of her own. The harm that women face can be physical or emotional, momentary or ongoing. These situations make us wonder, "What would I want someone to do if that were me, my friend, or my daughter?"

1. Tell me about a time when you helped remove a girl or woman from harm's way. What was the situation?

    »   How did you get involved?

    »   Did you just step in or were you asked to help?

    »   What did you do or say that removed her from harm?

    »   How did you feel at the time?

2. Imagine you are invited to speak to a class of college students about removing friends from harm's way. What would you say?

    »   How would you help them understand when it is appropriate to take action?

    »   What steps would you tell them need to be taken to intervene respectfully?

    »   What would you say to give them courage to speak up or take action?

    »   What would you tell them about protecting themselves?

4-6. Healthy Body Choices

Women encounter body choices throughout their lives. As we mature, so do our choices. As young girls, we choose how to dress, and how to care for ourselves when menstruating. Later, we choose with whom to hold hands, kiss, and make love. As young adults we may face choices related to religious baths, genital circumcision, birth control, or abortions. We may need to make choices about childbirth – natural, sedated, or cesarean section. Later in life, we have choices to make about aging with grace and end of life care.

1. Tell me about a body choice that was especially life affirming for you. What was the situation? What was the choice you made?

    » Who did you talk with as you made your choice?

    » How did the conversation help you make your choice?

    » How is this choice still alive and thriving in your life today?

2. Now recall a more challenging body choice, one that put you at odds with others or even your own values. What did you decide?

    » Who was with you as a companion at this time?

    » Who or what made this a challenging body choice?

    » How did that choice positively affect who you are today?

3. What body choices you are facing today?

    » With whom are you talking about your wishes and choices?

    » What, of all your options, is the healthiest?

    » What do you need to do to make the decision and act on it?

Aging with Grace

by Diane Farrell

We often hear the expression "aging with grace," but what does that really mean? Does it have something to do with our appearance, or the way we function and navigate the world as older women, or our spirituality, or something else? As women, we face particular challenges as we age, due to cultural pressures in a world that glorifies youthfulness.

After working with older adults for over 20 years in my practice as a teacher of the Feldenkrais® Method, I decided to learn more about the process of aging to help me understand my students, and navigate the challenges facing my 87-year-old mother. I also wanted to develop greater self-compassion for my own aging. I went back to school at the age of 57 to study gerontology and have gained invaluable knowledge about how we age and how sociological and psychological elements shape adult development.

I grew up with the inevitable decline narrative of aging. "Growing old is not for sissies." It was generally believed that there was nothing that could be done to prevent illness and mental deterioration as one got older. Based on research by people like Ellen Langer and Becca Levy, I have learned that this isn't entirely true. Our mindsets can shape our reality. Those who believe in inevitable decline will perform worse on tasks involving memory, mobility, and self-efficacy. Therefore, aging well can be determined to some degree not only by what we believe, but also by what we choose to focus on. Instead of dwelling on the losses that will certainly come as we begin to lose friends, family, and perhaps some of our abilities, we can choose to shift our attention to that which is still within our power to do and to give.

Generativity, the ability to contribute to the well-being of others outside of ourselves and our families, is an important developmental task of middle age and beyond. Beethoven is a wonderful example of this concept. He continued to bring his creativity to musical fruition even as he became increasingly isolated by deafness. The depth of his generosity never fails to humble and astound me! He left behind a gold mine for future generations even as he neared the end of his own time on this earth.

I believe that aging with grace includes trying to worry less about how we look as older women, and continuing to develop our gifts, our compassion (including self-compassion), and our generosity. Though it is not easy, we can move toward gerotranscendence, a state in which we become more and more interconnected with both the past and the future, as we are aware of being part of the ongoing flow of living and dying.

Remembrance is about the past. Witnessing has to do with the present. Action is movement into the future. Action is the way we live into a new reality, and when we act out of the authenticity of who we are as a people, as leaders, as human beings, we help create that new reality.

The Right Rev. Mary Douglas Glasspool

4-7. Safe Sex – At All Ages

While safe sex may have originally meant birth control to prevent unwanted pregnancies, it has come to mean staying safe from contagious, life-threatening diseases passed on through intimate contact. Once the concern of teenagers and groups of especially vulnerable people, talking about and practicing safe sex is now essential for people of all ages. For example, baby boomers ages 55 to 75 now have the highest incidence of sexually transmitted diseases in their lifetimes. Conversations about safe sex are important, intimate, and can be difficult, whether they are with a daughter, a son, or an intimate partner.

1. Tell me about a time when you had a meaningful conversation about safe sex. Who was it with? What made it meaningful?

    » What questions have you had about safe sex in your life so far?

    » Who answered them for you?

    » If you still have questions about safe sex, where would you go for reliable answers?

2. In your experience, what has been one of the best ways you have seen safe sex communicated and supported in your family, community, or other organization?

3. Thinking ahead to the next generation, imagine a world in which safe sex is not an issue. Tell me about it.

    » What would make this possible?

    » What two or three things can your community do now to move in this direction?

    » What can you do?

4-8. CARING FOR OUR BODIES

When we care for our bodies, our bodies care for us. A healthy body enables us to live well and to achieve our goals. It enables us to learn, excel, and fulfill our dreams. Our success and well-being both necessitate that we care for our bodies with good food, exercise, and sleep. Caring for our bodies enhances our capacities to realize our dreams and do good work in the world.

1. Recall a time when you felt especially healthy and vigorous. When was it? What was going on in your life?

   » What contributed to your well-being at that time?

   » What were you doing to care for your body?

   » What were you doing for relaxation and fun?

2. Describe a time when you and others clearly benefited from your good health. What was the situation?

   » Who else was involved?

   » What elements of your self-care contributed to your capacity to do good?

   » What did you learn about caring for your body at this time?

3. Suppose you could make three changes, large or small, to better care for your body and your well-being. What would you do?

   » What will you do today to make these changes a reality?

   » Who will you ask to support you?

   » When and how will you follow up to assess the impact of these changes?

A PRACTICE: THE POWER OF POSITIVE MOVEMENT

by Elaine O'Brien

The greatest part of my work life for nearly 40 years has been helping people connect to their bodies and at the same time connect to each other. We know that exercise keeps our bodies healthy, yet people often avoid it thinking it is boring. Running on the treadmill or swimming laps alone can be lonely. One excellent way to enjoy exercise is to connect it with someone or something else important to you, for example, family, friends, or a cause you care about. Here are some ideas for staying healthy, enjoying physical activity, and making a positive difference while you are at it.

Make it Fun and Playful: Movement is essential for survival. Enjoying movement is essential for thriving. It is never too late to start. My oldest student is now 100. She started lifting light weights at 89! Think positive thoughts about physical activity. How did you enjoy moving and playing as a child? How can you modify that for your age? Think fun, sports, dancing, hiking outdoors, or kayaking.

Find Your Rhythm of Exercise and Rest: Be physically active most days of the week. Aerobic exercise, exercising the large muscles of the body continually and rhythmically, is THE key to fitness. Aerobic activities like brisk walking, dancing, and hiking also boost brain health. If you're pressed for time, take 5 to 10 minutes and dance to your favorite music. Balance activity with sleep, rest, and relaxation. Pay attention to your circadian rhythms. Your body needs sleep and rest to be healthy

Make Friends as You Move: Teaching aerobic dance has personally grounded me, lifted me up, and brought me joy. I have made great friends as I teach around the world. I am in awe when I see participants strengthening their minds, bodies, and hearts. Fellowship and friendships are cultivated and flourish through moving together.

Optimize Your Energy. Vary your physical activities. Along with aerobic fitness, cultivate your muscular strength, endurance, balance, core, coordination, and social bonds. Stop while you still feel great. Leave your training feeling exhilarated, not exhausted. This boosts motivation and reduces the risk of injury. Exercise needs energy, so mindfully plan ahead to have healthy food available when you need it. I coach athletes to carry food with them so they can manage their intake and not reach for vending-machine food.

Move for the Greater Good: Use your healthy body to help others. My friends and I have *Walked for the Arts*, *Raced for the Cure*, run marathons to support people with arthritis, danced with elementary school students, and performed regularly for people at the local memory-care center. I am frequently inspired by the grace and power of people involved in positive movement.

When we come together in the spirit of fitness, fun, and fellowship and when we build body awareness, knowledge, strength, proprioception, and social bonds, we create a legacy of positive action, self-determination, and inspiration for others to follow.

4-9. Dress Codes, For Better or Worse

Dress codes help organize our worlds. Around the world, dress codes are used to define roles, status, power, and authority. A Girl Scout's uniform and badges show membership and achievements, a doctor's jacket and stethoscope signal capacity and authority, and a cleaning person's apron and gloves tell of willingness to work on behalf of others. While dress codes and uniforms may make life easier, they can also be constraining and a source of worry for girls and women.

1. Tell me about a time when you wore a uniform that delighted you. It helped you feel like you belonged and gave you a sense of pride. What was your uniform?

   » What did you like about it?

   » How did it made you feel included? Proud?

2. Recall a time when you challenged a uniform or dress code that was unfair or limiting. What was the situation?

   » What did you challenge?

   » How did you do it?

   » What positive results occurred?

3. Most of us have dressed up for Halloween or a costume party. What is your favorite costume? Why?

   » How does this costume reflect your strengths?

   » What about this costume energized you to be your best?

4. What do your answers to these questions suggest about designing fun and equal dress codes for young girls and boys in school?

4-10. Safe Spaces

Cities, schools, medical centers, and communities around the world are challenging the idea that the way women dress, walk, and talk invites abuse and makes them vulnerable to violence. Understanding that safety is in part a function of space, exemplary organizations and communities are leading social transformation by designing safe playgrounds, well-lit streets, and safe housing for elders. There is much we can learn from those who are actively creating safe spaces.

1. Think about and describe a place where you regularly feel safe. Where is it? What about this space makes you feel safe?

    » How do people interact in this space?

    » What about this space brings out the best of people?

    » How did this space come into being?

    » Who keeps it safe now? What do they do?

2. Imagine a world where women and girls are safe. They don't just feel safe. They are safe. Describe this world.

    » What would be different from our world today?

    » How would towns, schools, and housing be different??

3. What do your stories and dreams suggest that you might do to make your village, town, or city a safer space?

It is a biological truth that safety is almost always a prerequisite for the best in us to emerge.

Krista Tippett

⟳ A PRACTICE: A LIFETIME OF BODY CHOICES

This practice is an opportunity to reflect upon body choices you've made through your life, how they have influenced you and those who were with you along the way. Use it for self-reflection and journaling or in dialogue with a friend. Be gentle with yourself. The memories and stories you recall will come with emotions as well as insights. Be grateful.

1. What is your earliest body choice memory? Was it embarrassing or empowering to you as a girl?

2. Now recall a body choice during your teenage years. What was it? Who did you talk with about it? How did it impact your life and relationships at the time?

3. Recall a body choice that defined your twenties, perhaps in college or your first job. What wise counsel did you get or wish you had gotten?

4. For each of the decades that follow, your thirties, forties, fifties, sixties, and seventies, recall body choices you made. Were they easy or challenging? How did you feel about your body at the time? How did your decisions strengthen some relationships and harm others? How are these choices alive with you today?

5. In your eighties, and with good fortune, your nineties, what body choices have you made and will you face? How are you feeling about your body now as an elder?

6. It makes sense at any age to prepare for end of life, since we never know when it will come. What conversations are you having about your body choices? With whom are you having them? Do you feel supported in these conversations? What is most important to you about your body choices now?

WOMAN, WONDEROUS BEING

by Puno Selesho

Woman.
Wonderous being.

Do you know your colours?
Do you know that your very existence paints big bold strokes of glory?
Have you felt the wonder knitted intimately into your soul?
The gentle shades of beauty that you carry?

Dear lady, look left, look right, begin to marvel at this diverse sisterhood.
Know full well that the Beloved is seeking you out each and every day.

Dear girl, you reflect light!
It's your walk, your talk, your mind, your smile. It's that silly dance you do.
    The way you solve the tough equations, the way you paint.
It's in your hello, it's your vibe, it is your fragility, it is your strength.
In all of it, in all of you: is the evidence of God's love.

You are the fragrance of the Beloved.
Your name is the whisper of mystery.

Woman.
Wonderous Being.

Do you know your colours?
Do you not see all this light you are reflecting?

5

HEALING FROM RELATIONAL ABUSE

*Women and girls fleeing violence and sexual abuse
need safe haven and companionship for healing.*

Abuse against women and girls is epidemic. It is as prevalent in developed countries as it is in developing countries. The UN Commission on the Status of Women estimates that 35% of women worldwide have experienced some form of physical or sexual violence either by an intimate sexual partner or a non-partner; it is as high as 70% in some countries; 50% of women victims of homicide globally are killed by intimate partners or family members; and adult women account for 51% of all human trafficking, with women and girls accounting for 71%.

These statistics paint a grim picture. At the same time, they shine a light on millions of women around the world who have survived and gone on to thrive in spite of violence, abuse, and shame forced upon them.

For these women, life is a healing journey, one they cannot go on alone. Healing takes courage, self-compassion, and openhearted people as companions on the journey. For many women, it is a journey of faith and trust that there is a better way to live that is safe, free from censorship, criticism, and harm, and surrounded by people who care.

As the following example shows, a complex ecology of caring and compassionate relationships is needed to inspire and support healing from relational abuse.

Molly lived with one goal in mind. As soon as she turned 18, she was leaving home. She loved her mother, but she had to get away from the stepfather who had repeatedly sexually abused her ever since she was 12 years old. She remembered the people at the church she went to with her mother before they moved. These people were always kind and accepting. She stayed in touch with one girl her age living with her elder grandmother. They said she could live with them as long as she went back to high school and graduated. The day after her 18th birthday, she got on a bus, traveled north, and moved in with her friend and grandmother. She attended high school and went to church regularly.

The church people gave her a job working in their thrift shop. They took turns driving her to medical appointments, school, and work. Then she met Toni, a single woman in business and living with her parents. Toni took an interest in Molly and began helping her. She coached her to succeed in school, and she taught her how to drive and how to think and speak for herself. Toni also served as a successful thriving woman role model for Molly. Over time their relationship, love, and mutual respect deepened. Toni's parents, especially her father, are role models of safe, empowering, and protective parenting.

Today Toni calls Molly her daughter. With her support, Molly got her GED and is now taking community college classes. Both Molly and Toni are seeing therapists, Molly for post-traumatic stress and Toni for help parenting a teenager in transition! Molly lives with Toni and her parents who bought her first, very used, car to go back and forth to work, classes, and church.

Molly's story illustrates one healing journey, fortunately a successful one. As we all know, there are hundreds of thousands of girls and women who, like Molly, need companions on their journey of healing from abuse.

The questions, stories, and practices in this chapter invite dialogue and compassionate listening about sensitive topics to help you and others on your healing journey.

5-1. Telling Our Stories

Storytelling has long been recognized as a way of healing. Telling our stories and hearing the stories of others help us know that we are not alone, that we are not the only ones to have suffered abuse. Telling our stories helps us acknowledge anger and shame, then move forward on our healing journey with self-compassion. Telling our stories is a gift we can give to ourselves and to others.

1. Tell me about a time when you shared a story of injustice or abuse and were glad you did. What story did you share?

   » What lead you to share this story?

   » With whom did you share it?

   » How did they respond?

   » How did you feel?

2. Think about times when people have shared their stories with you. How did you let them know it was safe to tell their stories?

   » What did you do to be a good listener?

   » How did it feel to be trusted with their stories?

   » How did sharing stories positively affect your relationships?

3. Do you have a story you want to tell now? I am here to listen.

Every woman of my vintage knows what sexual harassment is, although we didn't have a name for it.... For so long, women were silent, thinking there was nothing you could do about it. But now the law is on the side of women or men who encounter harassment, and that's a good thing.

Justice Ruth Bader Ginsburg speaking to Nina Totenburg

5-2. SELF-COMPASSION

Self-compassion means accepting yourself just as you are. It means acknowledging your pain and suffering and at the same time, being kind to yourself and making self-care a priority. You are not responsible for abuse inflicted upon you, nor for your abusers. What happened was not your fault. You are, however, responsible for your own healing and well-being. Self-compassion fuels the fires of healing and success.

1. Tell me about a time when you experienced self-doubt and turned it into self-compassion and self-confidence. What was the situation?

   » How did you create this remarkable transformation?

   » Who supported and encouraged you? How?

   » What did you learn about yourself at this time?

2. How do you maintain self-compassion?

   » What do you do to keep yourself feeling good about yourself? Physically? Mentally? Emotionally? Spiritually?

   » How do you love yourself as a daily practice?

3. Imagine a world where women regularly feel and practice self-compassion. What would such a world feel like?

   » What would women be doing differently?

   » How would people care for each other?

   » How would they talk with each other?

   » How would schools and communities be different?

5-3. Surviving Abuse

From bullying to domestic violence, girls and women experience and survive abuse. Many suffer abuse from the very people who are supposed to take care of them – mothers, teachers, doctors, coaches, nurses, and babysitters. Nonetheless, they go on to live good lives, to succeed at work and to become kind, loving, and supportive women. They turn surviving abuse into a life of thriving.

1. Tell me about a woman you know, yourself or someone else, who survived abuse and is thriving now. What happened?

   » Who or what enables them to be kind and loving?

   » What do you most respect and admire about them?

   » How did they learn not to repeat patterns of abuse?

   » What can we learn from them to help other girls and women turn surviving abuse into a life of thriving?

2. Imagine it is ten years into the future. As you wake, you look around and see the world has changed for the better. Girls and women are being cared for and respected.

   » How is abuse recognized, called out, and dealt with?

   » What are people saying and doing to care for survivors?

   » How are women being helped and supported to grow from surviving to thriving?

   » How are girls treated at home and in schools?

   » What has happened to create peace and justice in the world?

5-4. From Victim Talk to Value Talk

The societal response to abuse – physical and verbal – is too often to blame the victim. Teachers, parents, police, and even friends say things like, "Why did you encourage that?" or "What were you thinking? You shouldn't have been there," or even, "Why did you upset him?" This leads women to keep abuse a secret, to silently blame themselves, and to identify and talk as victims. Healing occurs when we shift our talk from "They did it to me," to value talk about what we appreciate, envision, and intend to accomplish. Every conversation is an opportunity for healing by practicing value talk.

1. Using victim talk, tell me about a time when something happened to you that made you feel like a victim, perhaps an auto accident, illness, failure at work, or sexual abuse.

   » What happened to you?

   » Who was involved? Who or what do you blame?

2. Now tell me about the same situation using value talk. What was the situation?

   » What did you do to take care of yourself?

   » Who helped you? What did they do or say?

   » What did you do to help others?

   » What did you learn in this situation?

3. Reflect for a moment: what did it feel like to tell your story in two different voices, using victim talk and then value talk?

   » What can we learn from this to help ourselves and others heal from abuse?

   » How can you use value talk more often in your life?

A Beautiful Butterfly with Bright Blue Wings

by Alejandra León de la Barra

My mother was born with great beauty inside and out. She was strong, very generous, and had many gifts. She was a great soul and a bright spirit. When I looked at her, I would see a magnificent butterfly with bright blue wings. She was a warrior who fought for her needs, dreams, and desires, but she kept encountering a stone wall that prevented her from becoming her unique self. That wall was her own mother, my grandmother, another woman.

We come from an aristocratic family where norms and traditions were followed to perfection. My grandmother, the matriarch of our family, was the one who established and upheld these conditions.

Before my twin brother and I were born, my beautiful blue butterfly wanted to savor the world. She wanted to study medicine, to help people, and to write a newspaper section dedicated to children. She fell in love with and wanted to marry a tennis player and then a singer. Her mother, the matriarch, did not grant her these wishes. "Women should only work at home. Who are those men you believe you are in love with? They do not have the correct last name for our family," she would say.

So how did my brother and I come out of our cocoons and become butterflies? While my mother had her blue wings still in place, we shared love and kindness. I knew she was not well, but for me, she was a bright light. I was only six years old when I saw the brightness of my mother's wings start to lose their light. I saw and listened to painful words and actions directed toward my mother. I was sad and confused.

The matriarch got my mother to marry a man with the correct last name. He was divorced from someone else the same day. Now there was a masculine figure in the family.

What happened next? He became the king of the palace, and we women started falling apart, physically and emotionally. Our wings did not shine anymore. Sadly, my mother's wings fell off inside a white room where she was secluded. I tried with all my heart, spirit, soul, and conversations with God to hold onto my gifts and values, to be grateful, and to have both self-compassion and compassion for my mother. It was not easy living this way, being a child, not knowing if I would ever accomplish my own dreams. My guardian angel told me to keep my wings open, to never lose hope, to be strong, to dare, and to keep dreaming. So here I am.

I am grateful, even to my grandmother, the matriarch. As a mother of her time, she did what she thought best. I am grateful to my mother, my blue butterfly, who also did what she thought best. I believe every instance of suffering made us understand a little more what it means to be women without the support of men. What we didn't always understand was that if we supported each other, held each other, and shared kindness, our lives could have been a beautiful garden with butterflies of different colors and shapes, dancing to create a better world.

"When we affirm another's beauty, we affirm something that cannot be owned or drawn into the grid of small mindedness or emotional need. There is a profound nobility in beauty that can elevate life, bring it into harmony with the artistry of its eternal source and destination."

John O'Donohue

5-5. Making New Friends

Healing from abuse often requires letting go of unhealthy relationships and patterns of relating, such as saying yes just to keep another person happy, making excuses for the person who harmed you, or overworking to appear okay when you really need to cry a bucket of tears. When this happens, you may find yourself needing to make new friends and wondering how to do it.

1. Friendships take time and attention. Tell me about a friend or someone you know who seems to have a lot of friends.

   » What makes them a good friend?

   » What do you see them doing to attract and keep friends?

2. Friendships deepen as people do things together, get to know each other better, and celebrate together.

   » What friendship would you like to deepen?

   » Is there a club you can join, or an event you can attend with this friend?

   » What other ideas do you have to nurture this friendship?

3. Imagine it is one year in the future. You are meeting a cherished friend. Tell me about your friendship.

   » What do you enjoy doing together?

   » What makes this friendship healthy for you?

   » How has this cherished friendship developed over time?

   » How do you and your friend nurture your friendship?

5-6. FORGIVENESS

Women who have been abused and hurt all too often carry anger and resentment toward those who abused them, toward anyone similar to their abuser, and toward themselves. To forgive fully takes time and work. It is worth it. When we forgive, we become free of pain and suffering that weighs us down, interrupts our sleep, and interferes with our healthy relationships. Forgiveness can lead to an epiphany of healing, a lightness of being, and the restoration of relational trust.

1. Tell me about a small violation that you have forgiven. Perhaps a friend forgot your birthday or someone charged you too much for their service. What was the situation?

   » How did you forgive in this situation?

   » Why did you forgive?

2. Now think of a bigger abuse, something more challenging to forgive. Perhaps you were overlooked for a promotion or you were laughed at when you spoke up. What was the situation?

   » How did you forgive in this situation?

   » How did you avoid blaming others and yourself?

3. Now reflect on a situation that is almost unforgiveable, a time when you were physically or verbally abused.

   » How have you forgiven those involved?

   » Who and what helped you heal and restore your wholeness?

   » What can we learn from your stories to help others forgive?

⮑ A Practice: Forgiveness Ceremony

Perform this ceremony to forgive when you feel hurt by another emotionally, physically, or spiritually. You may do it alone or with a friend as a silent loving witness.

1. Sit comfortably with an empty chair across from you. Invite your spiritual self to be with you during this ceremony.

2. Relax and imagine the person you wish to forgive sitting in the chair across from you.

3. If possible, look into their imaginary eyes and say, "I give back to you all that is rightfully yours." Pause and breathe. Repeat this phrase three or four times, pausing to breathe between each statement.

4. Now say, "I bring back to myself all that is rightfully mine." Pause and breathe. Repeat this phrase three or four times, pausing to breathe between each statement.

5. As you breathe, reflect and listen to your inner voice. Be aware of what you are seeing or hearing that is returning to you.

6. Thank the other person. Imagine them leaving the chair.

7. Invite your spiritual self to sit in the now empty chair.

8. Now say, "I forgive myself for judging myself for … (fill in whatever comes to mind)." Pause and breathe. Repeat this phrase three or four times, pausing to breathe between each statement.

9. Thank your spiritual self and look around the room. Notice what you see, hear and how you feel.

10. Make notes in your journal and/or talk with your witness.

> *Through forgiveness we stand alive and connected to what is unfolding right now.*

Anita L. Sanchez

5-7. I'm Okay and I'm Vulnerable

Women who have been sexually abused, objectified, overlooked, or punished for being strong and having opinions of their own often find it hard to be vulnerable. We feel blamed, shamed, and betrayed by the very people who say they care. Whether physically or verbally violent, abuse is an assault to our sense of self. It makes us feel powerless. As a result, we may find it hard to feel okay about ourselves and at the same time acknowledge our pain. It takes time for women who have been abused to learn to trust and be able to say, "I'm okay, and I'm vulnerable."

1. Think of someone you know who comfortably expresses vulnerability. How do they do it?

    » What do they do and say?

    » What does it evoke in you when they acknowledge fear, insecurity or hurt?

2. Recall a time when you expressed vulnerability, when you were nervous or hurt and yet you knew you were okay. What was the situation?

    » How did you express your vulnerability?

    » How did others receive you?

    » How did it positively affect your relationships?

3. What would a classroom look and sound like if kids learned to express vulnerability and have empathy for each other?

4. Imagine a workplace where it's okay to say, "I know I can do this, but I am nervous and need help." How would it be different from where you work now?

Healing One Day at a Time

by Caroline Adams Miller

The waitress looked expectantly at my father as he prepared to tell her what my brother, sister, and I would be ordering for lunch. The Howard Johnson restaurant was a family favorite, specializing in all-American fare like spaghetti, hamburgers, and fries. I couldn't wait for the food. I'd been looking forward to this treat all day.

"The vanilla milkshake goes to the heavy one," my father said to the waitress, looking at me as he spoke.

In a flash, my entire self-concept shifted. I'd heard myself described in lots of ways in my eight years, but the adjectives had always been flattering: tall, helpful, smart, athletic, and funny. But heavy? I suddenly felt ashamed. Nothing was the same for me after that meal. I was now tagged as "heavy." My dad had said it in public, and everyone had laughed. I was bad.

In the Twiggy era of the late 1960's, anything other than lithe was considered heavy, and that was how I chose to see myself going forward because that's how my parents saw me. The damage was internal and fierce. I hated myself because I couldn't measure up to the standards my parents had set for me.

At 14, I all but signed my death warrant by succumbing to bulimia, which was sweeping the country. At Harvard, I got worse. The achievement of getting in had done nothing to soothe my troubled psyche, nor had it helped me to quit. I resigned myself to living with an addiction that had no cure and could kill me.

I was 22 and married when I hit my last bottom. My husband was shocked when I told him my secret and begged him not to hate me for being damaged goods. I'll never forget the look on his face when I shared my misery and asked for help. He was scared, too.

Thirty-five years later, I'm in long-term, unbroken recovery. I'm a miracle. My bone density scans are normal. My hormones became regulated, and I was able to give birth to three healthy children. Having unconditional love was what finally gave me the courage to go to a free self-help meeting for compulsive eaters in 1984. I found hope and people who told me to hate the disorder, not myself. I found role models. I gave back when I got stronger. I broke the silence around eating disorders, writing the first autobiography by anyone who had gotten better, and then the first book by anyone who stayed better for decades.

Healing the invisible scars left by my parents has taken decades of work. Hitting bottom so young has many silver linings. One is that I don't hate my body, which many adult women say is why they have held themselves back from going after desired professional goals. Another is that I don't care what I weigh. Not thinking about weight has given me the emotional energy to go back to school, get a master's degree, and give my children a female role model who is prouder of her books than her looks.

I'm 57 years old and my father died without ever uttering the sentence, "I love you." My mother is still alive and has never hugged me that I can remember. But that doesn't give me the excuse to hurt myself or relapse to the behavior that was once my response to trying to look good enough to please them.

Overcoming my eating disorder created my superpower: I know that regardless of any trauma that befalls me, I will always be able to heal, love, survive, and even thrive again, one day at a time.

"There's a powerful saying that sometimes we need a story more than food in order to live. They tell us about who we are, what is possible for us, what we might call upon. They also remind us we're not alone with whatever we face."

Krista Tippett

5-8. Saying "I Believe You"

One especially meaningful way we can support women, especially those who have experienced abuse, is to listen to their stories and to say, "I believe you." Abuse is often a one-two punch: first, the physical or verbal abuse, and second, the blaming and shaming of the victim. Listening to stories of abuse may not be easy, but it is essential for healing and restoring a person's dignity.

1. Recall a time when you listened to a story of abuse and were able to say, "I believe you." What happened?

   » How did the story make you feel?

   » How did you express "I believe you," verbally and nonverbally?

   » What did you say or do to demonstrate compassion?

2. Think of a time when you've been a victim of physical, sexual, or verbal abuse, and you were able to tell someone else who believed you. What happened?

   » Who have you told your story to?

   » How did they show they believed you?

   » What did they do or say that communicated their belief and support for you?

3. Imagine you have created a safe haven for women who have been abused, whether domestic violence, sexual trafficking, or conspiracies of religious silence. Tell me about it.

   » What happens in this haven?

   » What makes it emotionally safe?

   » What are people saying and doing?

   » How are women supporting women?

5-9. Being a Healing Companion

Women who have been abused need friends and companions to listen and hear their stories and to support them toward healthy decisions and relationships. Physical and verbal abuse is relational betrayal, a gross misuse of power that destroys women's self-esteem and trust in relationships. Often it takes a team, a community, or a circle of people to model healthy relationships for those who have suffered abuse. Being a healing companion is sacred work, an invitation to heal ourselves as we listen to and support another.

1. Tell me about a time when someone listened to you and helped you learn and become a better person. What was the situation?
   » What did they do and say that was helpful to you?
   » How did you feel when this happened?

2. Tell me about a time when you found yourself listening to someone's pain and suffering, perhaps their #MeToo story.
   » How did you feel to be a listening companion?
   » What did you say or do to bring out their best?
   » How did it affect your relationship?

3. Think about a woman you know who is a role model of healing companionship. Who is it?
   » How would you describe their style of relating?
   » What do they do to support others' healing?
   » What do you respect and admire about them?

A Practice: The Healing Power of Listening

by Kay Lindahl

One of the most valuable contributions we can make to someone who is hurting is the gift of listening – truly listening. We often wonder what we can say that will be most helpful, when it is really the *quality* of our listening that opens up the possibility for healing. There is a wholeness and a holiness to deep listening. It is not something we do. It is something we are. We become a listening presence, a way of being in which stillness and attentiveness provide the space in which someone can speak authentically and know they have been heard. Here are three simple practices that support the art of listening:

Become comfortable with silence. Take at least one minute each day to be still, to be quiet, to let go of all the doing, and to simply be. When someone stops speaking, ask them: "Is there anything else?" Then wait in silence for a few seconds. Your attentive silence lets them know that it's OK for them to pause for a moment and that it is safe to say more.

Get to know your inner voice. Ask yourself the question: "What wants to be said next?" rather than "What do I want to say next?" and wait for your inner wisdom to emerge. As you become familiar with this voice, you will discern when it's time to speak and when it's time to continue listening.

Learn to become present in the moment. Practice pausing and sensing your surroundings. When you turn lights on or off, open or close doors, get in or out of your car, pause. When you stand in line at the market or wait for an appointment to start, breathe. Notice the peacefulness that emerges in these moments.

The more time you commit to each of these practices, the greater your capacity to be a listening presence and a healing power communicating heart to heart.

MULTILINGUAL

by Medha Gupta

I speak Hindi: the language that unites the land of my people.
The land of waterfalls and new beginnings.
The land of mountains and hope.

I speak Bengali: a language considered to be one of the most beautiful
in the world.
The language of the twittering birds.

I speak Marathi: the language of the fierce warriors that drove the
colonizers away.
The language that roughens my mouth every time I speak it.

Yet when I speak English with an accent,
I become uneducated and uncivilized.

6

EDUCATING FOR SOCIAL CHANGE

The education of girls and women pays it forward forever.

The education of women and girls is a proven path to ending poverty, increasing economic prosperity, and enhancing global well-being. According to UNESCO, one additional year of school increases a woman's earnings by 20%. Women's health and children's health improve with education, as do overall survival rates. Child marriage and early pregnancy rates decrease as girls and women are educated.

Despite clear benefits, we have a long way to go until girls and women are fully able to participate in education. Almost two-thirds of the world's illiterate adults are women. UNESCO estimates 130 million school-age girls are currently out of school.

Around the world, schools and communities are responding with caring experiments to address barriers such as gender-biased teaching curriculums, poverty, unsafe conditions, sexual harassment, and abuse. Elk Hill, in Virginia, combines small classes, personal instruction, and counseling to provide students with the emotional and social safety needed to succeed academically.

Soon after being taken from an abusive home and placed in a foster home, Denna began at Elk Hill in 10th grade. She kept her head down, seldom made eye contact, and rarely participated in social activities. She spoke quietly, was difficult to understand, and was easily startled by loud noises. In frustration, she kicked walls and ran away from faculty and staff. Familiar with these signs of abuse, Elk Hill staff quickly wrapped her in social support services. They also noticed that many of her frustrations stemmed from her 6th grade reading level in a 10th grade class. She couldn't do it, so she didn't try. They provided personal one-on-one reading coaching, and her attitude soon changed. "Hold on, wait, don't tell me," she'd say, as the teacher watched her mouth form the words. She took her time… then her eyes would open wide and she'd say the word correctly with a smile on her face! By the end of 10th grade, she was reading fluently at 8th grade level. Two years later, she graduated with honors and is now successfully attending Virginia Commonwealth University, studying to be a reading teacher.

In addition to supporting and educating girls and women directly, schools are using education to change the social dynamics among girls and boys, among girls and their teachers, and within whole communities. As reported by JBI International, Safe Schools for Girls (SS4G) in Rwanda empowers girls to remain at school to complete upper secondary education and beyond, and it teaches boys to treat girls and women with respect. Its integrated approach embraces academic classes and support for socio-emotional and economic challenges faced by girls. It includes mentorship, a voluntary savings and loan program, a school scorecard, and an "engaged boys" program. Along with their traditional academic classes, boys have classes on how to respect and empower girls and women in their lives and communities.

As Safe Schools for Girls shows, educating girls and boys as equal and valued can transform the culture of a community from violence against girls and women towards uplifting, protecting, and empowering girls and women.

The questions, stories, and practices in this chapter are invitations to join with others to discover and dream of ways to transform schools to empower girls and women.

"I know of no better weapon in life to fight injustice than education."

Tererai Trent

6-1. LOVE OF LEARNING

Thriving women and girls are natural learners. They are curious and creative, always seeking to discover new knowledge and better ways of doing things. Some love to learn by reading, others through dialogue, and others by doing and experimenting. Whatever their learning styles, the love of learning energizes them, opens new doors, and gives them the knowledge they need to succeed in life.

1. Recall a time when you were caught up in the love of learning, a time when you were very engaged in learning. Tell me about it.

    » What were you learning?

    » Why was it captivating to you?

    » How did you approach learning at this time?

2. Think of a time at home, at school, or on the job, when you felt that you were learning well. What were you learning?

    » What about the situation made learning go so well?

    » Who or what made it interesting for you?

    » How did others support your love of learning?

    » How did you feel about yourself as you were learning?

    » How has that learning enlivened your life?

3. If I were to talk to some people who know you very well and I were to ask them about you as a learner, what would they say?

    » What would they tell me are your greatest gifts as a learner?

    » What would they tell me about ways your love of learning has had a positive impact on them?

6-2. Education Determination

For many girls and women going to school and acquiring an education is an act of determination, even sacrifice, for them and their families. Some mothers work two jobs to pay for their children's education. Girls in African villages walk miles to attend school or to have internet access. Working women attend night school or take online classes to further their education. Women who value learning are willing to do whatever it takes for an education.

1. Tell me about a girl or woman in your circle of friends or family who has been determined to get an education. Who is she?
   » Why do you say this about her?
   » What education does she seek?
   » Who or what supports her?

2. Recall a time in your own life when you were so determined that you overcame barriers to achieve an educational goal. What was your educational or learning goal?
   » Why did it take determination on your part to achieve it?
   » Who and what supported you?

3. Imagine a world in which all girls and women have access to safe, empowering education from kindergarten through college.
   » What is different about this world?
   » How are schools different? Teachers? Classrooms?
   » What new approaches to education have been introduced?

4. What one action will you take to enhance the education of girls and women in your community or the wider world?

Increasing Value by a Degree or Two!

by Jessica Cocciolone

"I was never told that college was an option." *That is what my mom said to me about her exposure to college as a kid. Her grandparents were immigrants. Both her parents worked, and so she was expected to work. She got married right out of high school and eventually had a child. After this marriage unraveled, there was another one with another baby, me. Unfortunately, my father passed away when I was 3. When I was around 7 years old, we began a new journey that eventually landed us in California.*

I don't remember exactly when my mom started going to college. I just remember a sense of it always being a part of my childhood, along with her working as waitress and raising my brother and me. My mom was working on a degree in fashion design. I got to dress up in the clothes and costumes she designed. To me, her school was like a never-ending dress-up party.

As I was starting the transition into high school, my mom was beginning a transition of her own. She was done with taking a few classes here and there at community college. She was now transferring to a full-time program at UNC- Greensboro. We packed our van and moved from sunny California to North Carolina. My mom continued to wait tables and study toward her future.

We never had much financially, but as a child, I was surrounded by love, family, and a community of women who supported us. I went to low-income schools where the majority of my friends' parents, many single moms, were not educated. I was never aware that my experience was different. I don't remember my mom ever really pushing me to go to college. That has never been her way. I learned the value of education by the way my mom lived. I understand now that watching my mom sacrifice to work her life around college instilled the importance of education in me. I decided on my own that not going to college was not an option. Finally, as I was preparing to graduate from high school, my mom was preparing to graduate with her Master's degree and start a career. My mother's life changed forever the day she obtained her MA degree. It has enabled her to travel the world, lead teams, and develop ideas that have been patented. It has transformed her life from being low-income to a solid upper-middle class American.

When it was my time to go to college, we didn't go on any college visits or look beyond our local community, but my mom was there to help me fill out the community-college paperwork and navigate the overwhelming financial-aid process. She was by my side encouraging me forward. Through her quiet and steady devotion to her education, she taught me that further education was not only possible, but would also open doors to worlds beyond, worlds that I never knew existed.

The world that opened to me because of college has been rich and full of interesting thoughts, people, cultures, and experiences. College and my life since have deepened my belief in the importance of education, especially for girls and women. My academic achievements, a BA and an MBA, have supported my passion and led me to advocate and work for increasing children's overall well-being. Education is at the heart of the matter.

Today, as I raise my 9-year-old daughter in a solid upper middle-class community, college is in her lexicon. At 6, she proudly announced that she will be attending our local university to get her degree while living at home. While her focus has changed from veterinary medicine to working with dolphins to running a hotel for dogs, her steadfast commitment to going to college has not.

6-3. Educating Girls for Leadership

A future of women in leadership, able to transform the social and economic well-being of communities and the world, starts with the education of girls for leadership. To have women of all backgrounds, races, and gender orientations in leadership requires the conscious and deliberate education of girls for leadership in our homes, schools, communities, and workplaces.

1. What opportunities, formal and informal, have you had to learn about and practice leadership? Tell me about one.

   » What did you learn about leadership?

   » What did people notice and affirm about you?

   » How did this situation shape who you are as a leader today?

2. Tell me about a school or organization that effectively educates girls for leadership. Who are they?

   » What leadership capacities do they teach?

   » How do they empower girls as leaders?

   » How do girls practice these leadership capacities?

3. Imagine a school with an exemplary and innovative program for educating girls for leadership. What are they doing?

   » What are they doing that is new and different?

   » What opportunities do they provide for girls to experiment?

   » How do they help girls learn from mistakes?

   » What mentoring and training do they provide?

4. Now, what one concrete step do you wish your local community would take to educate girls or women for leadership?

6-4. WORDS CREATE WORLDS

What students see, hear, and read via radio, TV, social media, schoolbooks, classroom curricula, and sacred texts conveys images and words that influence who they become. Words create worlds. They illustrate and teach social norms and gender expectations. At their best, schools ensure gender-free language, gender-equitable curricula, and positive roles models for all students. They use words and images to show respect and create self-confidence among all students.

1. Tell me about a book you've read that portrays women as positively powerful. What is it?

    » What language or story shows women held in high regard?

    » How did the author do this?

    » How does reading this book make you feel?

2. Think about your daily reading materials and TV shows. Which ones are most empowering for girls and women?

    » What makes them empowering?

    » What messages do they convey about women's positive potential and place in society?

3. Imagine you are on a national committee to revise the curriculum used in schools across your country.

    » How will you ensure that all students can read about themselves in the stories of the new curriculum?

    » How will you add women's wisdom to the curriculum?

    » How will you ensure that all students have positive role models with whom they can relate at school?

    » What else will you do to design an equitable curriculum?

How We Build Confidence

by Angela B. Koh

This is a story of my beloved student, Rachael, through whose journey I continue to learn much about educating for the future.

"I can't. This is too difficult," said Rachael, as she watched me play a new piece on the piano. Even at the tender age of five, Rachael was very clear about what she liked and disliked. She liked blue, and she disliked pink. She liked super heroes, and she disliked princesses. She liked playing the piano, but she disliked playing in front of others. She absolutely disliked making mistakes. A new piece meant that she would most likely make mistakes.

"But we can't only play the pieces we already know how to play. How can we get better without learning new stuff?"

"........"

I knew the awkward silence meant she wasn't convinced.

"Can I make a mistake?" she asked.

"Yes, of course!" I nodded. "Of course, you can totally make mistakes. That means we get to do it again. Wow, I would love that. Can we count how many times we get to repeat this?"

Reframing mistakes as something to value and even get excited about had not been my approach before that day, not for myself and not for my other students. But it seemed like a good strategy to encourage Rachael. Little did I know that this was a sound approach supported by research. Students complimented on their efforts tend to persist longer in the face of challenges than those complimented on their natural abilities, so-called talents, and outcomes.

That day left a clear mark in our learning journey. Not only did we transform our attitude about mistakes, we also made a small promise to ban phrases like "too difficult," "easy peasy," or "I can't!" We made a conscious choice to point out that anything new can feel difficult until

*it becomes familiar. Each time she finished learning a piece, I asked
Rachael questions:*

- *"Wow, this piece sounds really nice. How did you practice it?"*
- *"Would you say this is becoming easier for you to play well?"*
- *"What about two weeks ago when we started learning this piece?
  Was it easy then? Why do you think it is easier now?"*

*Rachael seemed to get it, and the twinkle in her eyes seemed to get
brighter as she answered my questions.*

*Fast forward five years. Rachael is ten years old now. She plays
advanced repertoires, has successfully completed a number of conser-
vatory exams, and has won various awards in competitions. But our
biggest accomplishment is not what we can see on a piece of paper or
show others on stage. It is what we know in our hearts. We know the
outcomes of honest and hard work. We are confident in what we know
and can do. We also know that there's a lot more that we haven't done
yet and don't know yet, but the key word here is "yet."*

*Today when Rachael comes to her lessons, she is ready to articulate
exactly what she worked on that week in preparation for the lesson. I
know these are invitations and permission for me to comment on her
progress, to notice the evidence of her hard work, and to celebrate it
with her. Not only that, if I ever become forgetful of my new role as a
progress detective and start teaching sections that she hasn't yet practiced, Rachael unapologetically informs me and requests more time so
she can have the joy of exploring and learning new things herself.*

*The ultimate goal of education is to foster independent learners who
can direct their own learning confidently and competently so that their
learning continues beyond formal education. I think Rachael has taught
me how to trust students' abilities and create a space where they can
safely experiment without fearing failures and judgments.*

6-5. Your Relational Compass

Schools dedicated to preparing girls and women to be leaders of their generations educate them with relevant knowledge and needed skills. They also foster the development of a *relational compass*, the orienting values, beliefs, and ideals that enable them to embrace and navigate the complexities of diverse relationships from childhood through adolescence to adulthood.

1. Tell me about your relational compass.

   » What are the values, beliefs, and ideals that guide your relational life and how you treat people?

   » What value or ideal helps you decide what to do in delicate situations or conflicts?

2. Recall how your relational compass developed over time.

   » What experiences shaped your sense of what is right and what is wrong when it comes to dealing with other people?

   » Whose voice do you hear in your head when you have to make a decision about what to do in a relationship?

3. Tell me a story about a time when you felt tested and your relational compass came in handy, helping you make a good decision. What was the situation?

   » What did you do or say?

   » How did you feel in this situation?

   » How did it positively affect your relationships at the time?

4. You have been invited to talk to a group of 13-year-old girls about the importance of having a relational compass.

   » What would you say to them?

   » What would you suggest they do to become clear about their own beliefs, values, and ideals?

6-6. POSITIVE RIPPLES OF EDUCATION

Education changes our lives and the lives of those around us. As we learn and transform, the changes we make are felt as positive ripples in our families and communities. Sometimes it is the knowledge we share that makes a positive difference. Sometimes it is our new earning power that enables us to better provide for our families. Often, the biggest positive ripple is that we become role models that encourage others to follow us on the path of education.

1. Tell me about a girl or a woman whose education was transformational and created positive ripples.

    » In what ways did education transform their life?

    » How did their education benefit their family?

    » How did it benefit the greater community?

2. Tell me about positive ripples of education in your family.

    » Who was the first woman to reach an educational milestone, such as high school or college graduation?

    » What challenges did they overcome along the way?

    » Who supported them and encouraged them?

    » What did they do as a result of their education?

    » How has their educational history affected your sense of what's possible?

3. Imagine you are invited to speak at a school that celebrates intergenerational learning. Grandparents, parents, and students will be in the audience. What story do you tell about ripples of education in your family?

    » Who or what are you most proud of in this story?

    » Who or what inspired you toward education?

6-7. Teachers and Parents Changing Things Up

Gender-role bias can be seen among girls and boys at an early age. In preschool, boys often choose to play with cars, making loud noises and crashing them together, while many girls choose to play with dolls, dressing them and having conversations with them. Whether this is biologically wired or learned behavior, adults can help children expand gender fluidity. For example, Ellen Barry in the New York Times reports that the preschool curriculum in Sweden urges teachers to change things up. In one school, boys learn to dance, and girls learn to yell.

1. Tell me about a teacher you know who has changed things up for girls and boys in their classroom. What did they do?

    » How did they make it fun for students?

    » How were parents engaged? School administrators?

2. Imagine a bold experiment for home or the classroom to help children explore alternative gender activities. What is your most creative idea?

    » What do you need to make this bold idea a reality?

    » Whose help will you need? How will you get it?

    » What is the first step you will take? When will you begin?

3. Holidays teach and reinforce social norms including gender expectations. You have been invited to serve on a committee to design and launch a new holiday dedicated to liberating gender expectations. What would you call this new holiday?

    » How will it be celebrated at school, at home, and at work?

    » What will be the key message of this holiday?

⟳ THREE PRACTICES: GENDER-NEUTRAL LANGUAGE

The following are a few ideas for creating meaningful disruptions in the way children learn about roles and identities.

1. **Empowering Students to Self-Identify**

   » Ask students to identify themselves on the first day of class. Ask them to fill out index cards with their preferred name and pronouns and whatever else they want you, other teachers, and their classmates to know about them.

   » Follow their writing with a discussion of the act of self-identifying. How did it feel? What surprised them? What are they curious about relative to their classmates?

   » Keep this information on file. Update it periodically, and share it with substitute teachers.

2. **Elevating Life and Career Possibilities**

   » As you address students, use words like scientists, readers, athletes, writers, and artists. Choose words that give them a sense that they are what they are studying.

   » Avoid using gendered language to address students, expressions such as "Ladies and gentlemen," or "Boys and girls," or "Guys."

3. **Grouping by Interests, not Genders**

   » To help students learn about each other and respect the diversity in their class in a light way, use fun categories to create small groups in your class. For example, you could form groups based upon birthdays, ice cream flavours, pet preferences, or number of siblings.

   » Avoid grouping students by gender, unless the purpose of your activity is teaching inclusion and exclusion.

6-8. School Cultures of Gender Safety and Equity

Creating a school culture that values gender safety and equity requires strategic and systemic transformation. Exemplary schools design gender equity into all aspects of the school culture: pedagogy, practices, programs, policies, and structures. The traditional culture in which the voices of the principal, teachers, and students are respected in that order is eclipsed by open communication and collaboration.

1. Tell me about a time when you felt safe and equal at school.

    » What made it a safe and equal culture for you?

    » How did you feel there?

2. Imagine that you are speaking to parents, students, faculty, and administration of a school in need of transformation. What do you say are the three keys to creating gender safety and equality?

    » What do you tell educators they can do?

    » How about parents? Administrators?

    » What story do you tell to illustrate that positive change is possible?

3. Imagine, one big dream, an exemplary school or classroom, where girls and women feel safe and equal. What is the school?

    » Tell me about a day in a classroom.

    » Describe the relationships among educators and students.

    » What conditions create moments of thriving for the girls and women who are part of this school?

    » What is the boldest experiment being conducted in this school to teach positive gender awareness?

    » In what ways is gender equity designed into the school's practices, policies, and structures?

6-9. Thriving School Community

At its best a thriving school is a community where everyone learns, grows, and has opportunities to discover their interests and strengths. It is a center of learning that brings out the best in everyone: students, parents, teachers, staff, and visitors.

1. Tell me about a school that you experience as a thriving school community. Describe the school.

    » Who and what create conditions for thriving? The programs, policies, curricula, facilities, faculty, and staff?

    » How does it bring out your best? The best of students?

2. Imagine now that it is ten years in the future. You awake from a long sleep and see that your local school is just as you always wished it would be. What is different at the school?

    » What are people saying and doing?

    » How are they treating each other?

    » How would you describe the school culture?

3. A journey of one thousand miles begins with one step. What is the first step you will take in your school community to bring your dreams to life?

4. Now imagine an even bigger and bolder step involving more people. What ideas do you have to sustain the excellence of school communities around the world for generations to come?

➲ A PRACTICE: FAVORITE COLORS

At the age of three, children start defining themselves and become curious about differences among people. Their favorite color is one form of self-definition. Then around school age, boys and girls start associating their preferred color with their society's gender norms. Suddenly a boy who liked pink associates that color with girls and no longer finds it his favorite. By age 7 or 8, social norms about what colors are right and wrong based on gender have been considered and assimilated. The following conversation about colors can help students understand gender stereotyping.

1. Ask all students to write their favorite color on a piece of paper.

2. Going around the room, have each student say their favorite color.

3. Have the entire class form groups based upon favorite colors.

4. Ask the groups to discuss the following:
   » Why is (shared color) your favorite color?
   » How does the color make you feel?
   » Who or what does the color remind you of?

5. Now ask everyone to look around the room. Ask and discuss:
   » What do you notice? How does it feel when you like a color that is different from a friend?
   » How do you think or feel when you see that a boy's favorite color is pink or a girl's is blue? Why do you feel or think this way? Why does it matter?

6. Conclude by pointing out that we often stereotype people based on their gender, the things we think boys and girls are supposed to be. Explain that stereotypes aren't very accurate. When we look around the room, we see that girls and boys like all colors.

SAK SAUM

by Ginny Hanson

Sak Saum means to restore dignity, value, and beauty. The deepest change happens as people are empowered to make their own choices. Therefore, we train people to become successful business owners within their own homes and self-made groups.

While visiting orphanages in Phnom Penh, in 2002, we heard children crying out, "If my mom had a job, she would not have to work as a prostitute," and "If my father had a job, we would be a family." A seed was planted in our hearts. We started with one mom, one sewing machine, and one precious baby who would grow up to have a bright future. Since then we have created safe and sustainable sources of income for hundreds of survivors of human trafficking and exploitation to work, grow, and learn.

Without choice, it is not love. Without love, there is no change.

7

LEVERAGING FINANCIAL SAVVY

Financial savvy empowers women to lead the economies
of their lives, their communities, and the world.

Financially savvy women are intentional about how they make money and how they use it. They balance spending, saving, and giving in alignment with their values and dreams. They are willing to work hard, and they expect to receive equal pay for equal work. They account for expenses, profit, and loss as measures of their financial well-being. They are comfortable talking about money and negotiating financial agreements that ensure fairness and equality.

Women's access to money, entrepreneurship, rights of ownership, and positions of power in financial institutions vary from country to country. Women have been, and in many parts of the world still are, excluded from monetary affairs. Women's success, however, demands that they become financially savvy, able to understand and apply the basics of money management, wise financial decision-making, and sustainable economic principles.

Cultural norms often prescribe that women share their wealth and financially look after their extended families. This can be both a blessing and a burden. Women have proportionately less to give, being paid on average 80 cents for every dollar paid to men, and yet they invest a higher portion of their earnings to support others. Families and communities benefit as women develop and leverage financial savvy. The Women's Global Empowerment Fund (WGEF) in Uganda empowers women with business training and access to microloans. As a result of WGEF, five women ran for and won political office in Uganda in 2016. Similarly, Friendship Bridge in Guatemala offers entrepreneurial training and microcredit loans to teams or "trusts" of women. Such micro-economic programs illustrate the efficacy of financially savvy women. When women have money, they buy chickens and cows that feed the community and provide a financial return. Women use their financial resources to ensure their families and communities thrive in the US as well. There are dozens of Meet Up groups dedicated to clipping coupons. With names like Coupon Trading, Frugal Living, and Coupon Moms, these groups meet online and face-to-face to share coupon resources and best practices about how to find and use coupons to save money for themselves and their families.

An Ernst & Young report describes women as an overlooked talent resource and source of economic potential. It suggests that tapping into the full economic potential of women would be equivalent to having an additional one billion people in business and in the workforce contributing to the global economy and sustainability. Women, they claim, are the next emerging market with potential to foster global income growth in the range of US $13 trillion to $18 trillion and be significantly influential in politics, business, and society. The potential is great, and so are the questions it raises. How can women be the next emerging market and benefit from it, rather than be exploited by it? What do women need in order to take charge of the economies of their lives, communities, and the world?

The questions, stories, and practices in this chapter are invitations to dialogue about what financial savvy means to you and how you can leverage it for the good of your family, community, and the world.

True wealth is created when an individual or likeminded people act with an intention to create value and add to the beauty, joy and peace in the world around them.

Verna Allee and Dinesh Chandra

7-1. Financial Savvy

Financially savvy women are intentional about how they make money and how they use it. They understand how to balance spending, saving, and giving to achieve their goals and dreams. Financial savvy means keeping track of financial wellness, being comfortable talking about money, and negotiating financial agreements to ensure fairness and optimal financial return in family and work settings.

1. Tell me about your financial savvy. What aspects of finance and money management are you especially good at?
   » How did you learn these financial skills?
   » Who helped you or gave you useful advice? What was it?
   » Tell me about a time when you used your financial savvy and the results were better than you had hoped for.

2. Rate your financial wellness on a scale from 1 meaning it needs urgent care to 10 meaning it is vibrantly healthy. How do you stand today?
   » What does financial wellness enable you to do or not do?
   » What do you do to maintain financial wellness?

3. Who is a financially savvy role model for you? Why did they come to your mind?
   » Tell me a story that illustrates their financial savvy
   » How do others benefit by their financial savvy?

4. Imagine that it is your job to teach kids about financial savvy by helping them run a lemonade stand. What are your three key lessons for them?

Money Values into Action

by Amanda Trosten-Bloom

When our daughter was five years old, my husband and I began giving her a weekly allowance. It was a relatively small allowance, but substantial for her. Searching online to see how different parents handled this, we found a process that made sense to us.

It began with a conversation between the two of us. Which of our values did we want her to learn? We wanted her to experience limited financial autonomy, to practice living within (somewhat) limited means, and to learn to save and give as well as spend.

To facilitate her understanding, we divided her allowance into three separate envelopes. The first was her spending envelope. Containing 70% of the whole, this became her disposable money for day-to-day expenses. She could spend this on anything she wished, even things we normally discouraged her from having like candy or plastic jewelry – nothing illegal!

The second, her saving envelope, contained 20%. It could be used to buy large items over time that she otherwise could not afford, such as a new stuffed animal or a CD with music that she loved. She often carried this money with her on vacations so she could buy a souvenir of her travels. We agreed to match whatever she put into savings and left there for a month or more in order to instill the concept of earning interest.

The third, her giving envelope contained her tithe or 10%. This money was explicitly set aside for charitable causes that mattered to her. One time she used it to buy a Christmas gift for a child who had no mother. Another time she handed her entire envelope to a homeless person we passed on the street. Having money to give brought her joy. It began a pattern that continues to today. Now, at 25, she carries food in her car for people on the street and regularly donates time and money to charitable causes.

I'm grateful that we began this conversation she was so young. It has made her transition to financial independence easier for her and for us. It has made her a responsible and caring member of society. I am proud of her and how she uses money to care for herself and to help others.

Twenty Years Later

by Hannah Joy Bloom

The allowance system my parents created helped me learn from a very young age how to think about money over the long term. I quickly grew to understand that I needed to save up my money and think ahead so I could buy something that was really meaningful to me. Being able to save up and then donate some money to charity was always so energizing for me as well. It got me excited about giving from a young age because I felt good giving something that I had worked for to someone else. It also helped me learn how to research causes that were important to me.

All of these skills are now very important to me as a young adult, and I can tell you without question that I was always ahead of my peers when it came to understanding how to handle money.

7-2. Personal Relationship with Money

We all have a relationship with money. For some of us, it is a serious relationship. We work hard, earn, and save. For others, money is an elusive wind always blowing just out of reach. For still others, money is power, the means to get what we want and to influence the world around us. For most of us, our adult relationship with money reflects our inherited narratives about money, the messages we heard about money as we grew up.

1. What were the most common messages you heard about money as you grew up? What did you overhear parents, relatives, and other adults saying about money?

    »   What were you told directly about money?

    »   How do you remember people treating money?

    »   What did that teach you?

2. What is your first memory of saving money? Did you have a piggy bank or perhaps a savings account passbook?

    »   Who gave it to you?

    »   When or how often did you feed the piggy or go to the bank?

    »   What did you do with the money you saved?

    »   How did this influence your current financial habits?

3. Recall a time when the amount of money you had increased. For example, you got a raise, sold something, or got a gift.

    »   What happened?

    »   How did you feel about money at the time?

    »   What changed?

4. How would you describe your relationship with money now?

☯ A Practice: Sharing Views of Money

Everyone has unique attitudes, values, and experiences with money. This practice is an opportunity for two or more people to share life experiences and opinions about money, and if they wish, to create a list of shared guiding principles about money.

1. Take turns interviewing each other for 15 minutes using the following questions. Make notes as you go.

   » What role has money played in your life? What has it enabled for you, your family, and your community?

   » Tell me a story about the way having or not having money has influenced your life. How has this affected your relationship with money?

   » What does your culture, spiritual tradition, or heritage teach about the meaning of money and wealth? What quotation, sacred passage, or ritual best conveys this?

   » What do you see as an important guiding principle about money? Why is this important to you?

2. After the interviews, share and discuss the following:

   » I was surprised to learn this about you:

   » What we both seem to value about money is:

   » Our thoughts about money seem to differ relative to:

   » Three ideas about money that would help our relationship are:

While the exact origins of money are unknown, all its early forms were deeply related to the mysteries of the sacred.

Bernard Lietaer

7-3. Money of Our Own

For many women, being our own person means having our own money, earning it, saving it, using it, and giving it away as we wish. Ownership – of money, property, vehicles, or cell phones – is empowering. Having resources and money enables us to care for our families, achieve our goals, and contribute to our communities. It prompts us to use money wisely and to be authors of our own lives.

1. Tell me the story of your first money, whether you earned it or received it as a gift. It was your money to do with as you saw fit. What was the situation?

   » How much money was it? How did it come to you?

   » What did you do with it?

   » How did you feel about having your own money?

2. Why is it important for you to have money of your own?

   » What does it enable you to do?

   » How do you receive your own money?

   » How do you care for your money so that it will be there when you need it?

3. Tell me about your financial goals, the goals you set for money of your own.

   » What was your first earning goal?

   » How did you celebrate when you achieved it?

   » What are your savings goals now?

   » What are your giving goals now?

   » How do you use your money to help the world?

7-4. Investing in Ourselves

Women who value themselves invest in themselves. From small rewards for a job well done to big investments in education, homes, and even vacations, investing in ourselves pays off. Having financial grit, that is, persistently saving and spending for our goals and dreams, as well as helping others, is one way that we take care of ourselves, learn, and grow to be our best.

1. Think of a time when you were persistent and passionate about saving to do something you wanted to do or have something you wanted to have. What did you save for?

   » How did you feel as you saved?

   » How did investing in yourself positively affect your life?

2. Tell me about a time when you celebrated a success with a small reward. What was your success?

   » How did you reward yourself?

   » How did the reward reinforce your self-confidence?

3. When have you made a big investment in your future? Maybe you went back to school, took a class, or bought a house. What was the investment?

   » What led you to make this investment?

   » How did it pay off in your life?

4. What would you tell a woman who is contemplating a big investment in her future about why it is important to do so?

7-5. Asking for Equal Pay

Women's pay is determined by what they ask. In all professions, including frontline employees, consultants, landscapers, plumbers, and managers, women establish their pay ranges by what they ask for. To be paid equally, women need to know their worth and ask for it. They need to learn salary, pay, and wage structures in order to ask for equal pay. For many women, it takes courage to talk about money and double courage to ask for equal pay.

1. Recall a time when you had a courageous conversation about money and got what you wanted. Maybe you asked for a raise, or equal pay, or perhaps you negotiated the price of a car. What was the situation?

    »   What did you ask?

    »   How did you know what to ask?

    »   Who coached you or encouraged you?

    »   What did they say or do?

    »   How did you feel at the time?

2. Now, imagine an organization, a business, a school, or a government agency that is fully committed to equal pay. Tell me about it.

    »   How would salary discussions be different?

    »   What financial information would be shared? How?

    »   How would equal pay positively influence productivity? Relationships at work? Morale?

7-6. Women Trading in the Marketplace

Trade, an important part of an economy, occurs in different forms in different cultures around the world. Whether it takes the form of buying and selling or bartering, trade communicates the value people see in what everyone brings to the table. The challenge for women who have been abused and objectified, and whose contributions have long been taken for granted, is to know their own value and the value of what they offer the marketplace.

1. Tell me about trade activities that are happening actively or regularly in your life. What do you trade and with whom?

    » What purpose does this serve in your life?

    » What is life-giving about these activities?

2. Let's call what you bring to the marketplace your trade. What values do others see in your trade?

    » Is it different from how you regard your own trade?

    » What might you do or say to enhance the perceived value of your trade?

    » How comfortable are you making a profit from your trade?

3. If you are already comfortable and competent with making a profit, explain how you learned this.

4. If you are not yet comfortable or competent with commercial activities that make a profit, what might give you the permission to embrace making a profit as life-giving?

FROM TRADED TO TRADING

by Angela B. Koh

These are true stories of women being used as the very object of trade, ugly and violent trade that robs women's dignity, rights, and even life. The gravity of the issues that surround stories like these is disheartening and overwhelming. But while it may feel daunting to imagine a solution that would put an end to these tragic stories, hope is closer than we might think, as shown in the sequel to each story.

Baby Samantha's Story: *Samantha is baby number six. Her mother, who earns her living as a prostitute in the Philippines, has forced her eldest daughter into prostitution, selling off the others in infancy. Women living in extreme poverty can see even their own babies as sources of income. The fact that the baby may be in the hands of heartless sexual predators is negligible against the need to survive. In a world where being born a girl can be a threat to safety and well-being, Samantha seems predestined to follow her sisters.*

Sequel – Baby Samantha and Manuel Deldio: *Manuel Deldio is an attorney practicing corporate and business law whose passion is to solve complicated corporate issues and implement operational frameworks. When he was approached by Rohei Foundations to help set up an adoption agency in Manila, he didn't see how putting a few babies in new homes each year would fight an issue that is so guarded by drug lords, pimps, and sexual predators. Then, getting a close look at these tiny girls, he questioned his own beliefs about what is meaningful and his own ability to make a difference. When Manuel met baby Samantha, his heart was lit up with the desire to save a life. He decided to adopt Samantha himself, although he was single and knew little about raising a child. He reached out for help, and a community of people came together: his family, friends, neighbors, and even his clients. There is a saying that it takes a village to raise a child, but it was really a case of a child raising a village.*

Khadija's story: *Khadija was killed to protect her family's honor. Marrying for love is not only forbidden for women in some cultures, but is also considered an act of shame, punishable by death. But honor was not all that Khadija brought home by dying. Her death brought home money to buy food for the family, as honor killing, a centuries old practice that murdered countless women to restore men's honor, has become a business activity that exchanges life for a ransom. So, the family received ransom to spare the life of the boy that Khadija had married, while even the slightest memory of Khadija's existence was to be wiped from this world, her name never to be called again.*

Sequel – Khadija inspired her cousin, Khalida Brohi: *That Khadija was killed is an irrevocable truth. But her cousin, Khalida, who lived through this gruesome murder, became a women's rights activist and educator. Khalida speaks boldly and loudly to raise aware-ness about women's issues with people of her own culture and beyond. She has spoken on world stages including TEDGlobal, Davos, and the World Affairs Council. Khalida brings hope and freedom to tribal women by way of education and training. She established the Sughar Foundation, Sughar meaning "skilled and confident women" in Urdu. The Sughar Foundation helps women learn about their rights and develop entrepreneurial skills to transform their treasured traditions, such as embroidery and arts, into businesses that empower women to lead trade and not be traded.*

Khalida's work has threatened her safety and health at times, includ-ing countless threatening calls and emails, a bombing in her office, and seizures from overworking. But she is fearless and restless until all women have an equal seat at the table.

7-7. MONEY COURAGE

It takes courage to leverage financial savvy, to ask for what you are worth, to invest in your education or the stock market, and to give generously to a cause you support. It also takes courage to say no to family members in need, to stop using credit cards when you know you don't have money, and to tell your children you can't afford things they want. Financial savvy means having courage to make choices congruent with our values and within our budgets.

1. Tell me about a time when you called on your courage and took a financial risk that paid off. What was the situation?

    » What did you do that felt like a courageous risk at the time?

    » How did you know it paid off? How did you feel?

2. Some of our biggest financial risks are times when we say no. Tell me about a time when you courageously said no about money to someone. What was the situation?

    » What led you to say no?

    » How did you do it? How did you feel when you did it?

    » What has been the positive impact of your courage to say no?

3. What is going on in your life right now that is calling for financial savvy and money courage?

    » What decisions do you need to make?

    » Are they related to your age? Your family? Your work?

    » Who can give you advice about these decisions?

    » What is your hope for ways the best financial decisions will play out in your life?

7-8. SPIRIT OF GENEROSITY

Thriving women are known for their spirit of generosity. We care for others financially, as well as socially and emotionally. We help people living with hunger, fear, and abuse and people dependent upon the generosity of others for their most basic needs by generously giving money, time, and other resources. As we tap into a spirit of generosity the world becomes whole and holy.

1. Tell me about a time when your spirit of generosity came to life, and you acted on it. What was the situation?

    »   What did you do? What did you give?

    »   How did your generosity help others? How did they respond?

    »   How did you feel when you did this?

2. Tell me about someone whose spirit of generosity you admire. Who is it? What makes you say they are generous?

    »   Tell me about an act of generosity that left a positive impression on you.

    »   Why was it so impressive?

3. Tell me about your regular giving. What are your favorite gifts to give?

    »   What causes do you support financially?

    »   How do you feel when you are generous?

4. If you had enough money to make one change in the world, what would it be? Why this change?

7-9. TALKING ABOUT MONEY

Financially savvy women are comfortable talking about money. They have people with whom they regularly talk about money and to whom they can turn for financial advice. They keep informed about their own finances from pay to savings to investments, and they stay up-to-date with world affairs and economic implications. Talking about money helps them have the information they need to negotiate wages, to create budgets, and to save in order to realize their goals.

1. With whom do you regularly talk about money?

   » How do these talks help you care for your own finances?

   » How do these conversations empower you?

   » Who initiates these conversations?

   » How do you participate?

2. Tell me a story about a money conversation that made a positive difference in your life. What was it about?

   » Who else was involved?

   » What was the outcome of this conversation?

   » How did it positively influence your life?

   » What did you learn from this situation?

3. What organizations or programs that you know are especially good at helping girls become comfortable talking about money?

   » Who are they?

   » What do they do?

   » What do girls learn?

7-10. The Sharing Economy

As the world changes, so too do currencies and means of exchange. The digital age has ushered in the *sharing economy*. Libraries now loan kitchen and garden tools, seeds, and video equipment along with books. With the many apps available, we can easily share cars, houses, boats, and even clothes. The sharing economy creates opportunities for us to generate income, to reduce our costs of living, and to meet new people around the world.

1. What sharing services do you use? How do they make your life easier and less expensive?

2. Tell me about ways that you share time, space, technologies, knowledge, or anything else with others. What has been especially meaningful for you?

   » What gave you the idea to do this?

   » What draws you to this sharing activity?

   » How did you make it happen? With whom?

   » What are some of the most positive results of this sharing?

3. What advice would you give to others wanting to join the sharing economy?

4. Imagine now that your community decides to open a sharing laboratory as an experiment in sharing. What would it be like?

   » Who would be involved? In what ways?

   » How would it benefit your community?

   » What would make it really fun to do?

My Mother the Banker

by Diana Whitney

Memories of my mother abound. She played hooky by hiding and reading under the front steps until her mother went to work. She read the encyclopedia from A to Z and was called by our local library when they got new books she might read. She tended me through polio, surgery, and mean-girl bullying at school, never letting on that I was different from my brothers and laughing when I climbed trees so high that I could not get myself down. She was a good cook and a good storyteller. When she wanted time alone, she reminded us of pirates who had roamed our land and buried treasures, telling us to go dig and see what we might discover. She regularly drank tea with her few, but lifelong, women friends. She began life adapting to gender roles and ended it her own financially independent person. She was a bookkeeper turned wife, and later a receptionist turned bank manager and corporate officer. As you can imagine, I became who I am in large part because of her, my mother the banker.

After she and my dad divorced, Mom got a job as a receptionist in a local bank branch. She easily made friends with colleagues and customers. She was the first person that customers saw and interacted with upon entering the bank. For many, she was the bank. She and the job were a good fit. She was financially savvy. Her ease with people and finances was a win, win, win, benefitting the bank, its customers, and our family.

Within a year she was promoted to assistant teller and soon to teller. She liked the work. When I asked her what it was like to handle money all day long, she commented, "It's no different than giving out tickets at the movie theater. You keep track of what you have, what people give you, and what you give them." The message was clear, her job was not about the money, it was about making life easier for customers. She went on to say that money was just paper. After a few days as a teller, it didn't seem much different from monopoly money! But of course, bankers needed to be unquestionably honest. At the end of every day, every penny needed to be accounted for. Honesty was a daily practice.

Within another year Mom was again promoted, this time to assistant bank manager, and soon thereafter to branch manager. I wondered why her friend Teresa, who had been a bank teller longer, did not get the job. Mom said that she, Teresa, and Irv, the incumbent bank manager, made the decision together. Teresa didn't want the job, so Mom became the branch bank manager, with Teresa as her righthand teller and Irv as her champion in the corporate office. They were a great team, demonstrating the value of transparency around money and communication.

Mom proved herself as a woman in a man's job. Within a year, she was appointed to the board as the first woman officer of the bank. The corporate office made a big deal of it, with celebrations at Mom's branch and the corporate headquarters. The pride I felt at the time lives with me to this day.

Mom led the bank through a decade of growth, directing the opening of several new branches and overseeing the turnaround of another. After experiencing a "just like on television" bank robbery and nurturing her team through recovery, Mom was ready for a change. She and her second husband, moved to Florida where she became a realtor and a force for social justice, selling homes to people of color when no other realtor would represent them.

Teresa, Irv, and Mom remained friends, exchanging letters until Irv passed, and then Mom at 92. Their legacies are interwoven into wisdom that I carry as an entrepreneurial woman, expressing myself through work, balancing relational and financial savvy, and contributing to a world that works financially for all.

Women's Work

By Erin Bad Hand

I thought I'd be able to write a
   poem about women's work
What we DO
I thought it would be a
   beautiful inspiring garden
   of a place
With magic, flowers everywhere,
   healing herbs, powerful songs
   and truth
How we hold the world cupped in
   the palms of our hands
But
I sit down to write, in the late
   hours of the night
When my babies are all finally
   asleep and the house
Is still a wreck but quiet
And I cannot summon the
   words
Can't force it, or find my
   garden…

What I've come to is that
Women's work
My work
The work of living
Is a garden, it is a song, it is
   healing

Though not at all
   always the beauty I find myself
Imagining it should be

There is so much strength in the
   work of rising
Of facing the day, of tending to
   beloveds
Of tending to children, life
   partners, plants
And animals
Of tending to yourself

And as the world keeps tracing
   the arc of a distant sky
Women keep rising
To do the work of living
To be love
To fully embody compassion,
   empathy and strength
And beauty and trauma and pain
   and rage and light

Women are doing that
Every day
We are singing our songs
We are tending our gardens of
   daily life, magic and all

8

WORKING FOR THE GREATER GOOD

Thriving women are a powerful, unstoppable force of social transformation creating a world that works for all.

Thriving women disrupt expectations. They succeed in their own ways, and in so doing, they chart new directions for women working for the greater good. This is certainly the case for the 36 women who joined the US House of Representatives in 2019. They include the first Muslim woman, the first Native American woman, and the youngest two women ever elected to congress. But that is not why they ran for office. According to Representative Ayanna Pressley (D-Mass), speaking to POLITICO, "None of us ran to be the first anything. We ran to make a difference. We ran to make change."

Another inspiring group of women succeeding on their own terms is Zimbabwe's *Akashinga* or Brave Ones. Described by the BBC as Africa's first armed, all-women anti-poaching unit, it is arresting poachers and changing the way animals are protected without firing a single shot. Akashinga is a community-based organization empowering marginalized women from remote villages to restore and manage large networks of wilderness to prevent trophy hunting.

In the art world, The Guerilla Girls is an anonymous group of feminist female artists working to fight sexism and racism by making art that is consciously disruptive. In their own words, "We wear gorilla masks in public and use facts, humor and outrageous visuals to expose gender and ethnic bias as well as corruption in politics, art, film, and pop culture." Their world-changing art has recently been seen in street and museum projects at the Tate Modern in London, the São Paulo Museum of Art, the Van Gogh Museum in Amsterdam, the Museum of Military History in Dresden, and Art Basel in Hong Kong.

Much is written about the value of women at work. Popular media and business journals regularly describe the benefits of women in the workplace, on boards of directors, and as CEOs. A Center for Creative Leadership (CCL) report by Cathleen Clerkin based on interviews with almost 750 leaders, offers compelling evidence for the value of women in the workplace, "Fortune 500 companies with the highest representation of women on boards financially outperform those with fewer women on boards. Moreover, gender-diverse teams have higher sales and profits compared to male-dominated teams." The CCL report goes on to say, "having more women in the workplace actually makes an organization a better place to work, is positively related to employee engagement and retention, and is associated with positive organizational outcomes for both men and women." As this shows, women make a positive difference in the workplace.

Working women are, at the same time, often described as an unrealized potential. A McKinsey Global Institute report estimates that $12 trillion could be added to the global GDP by 2025 if women's equality at work were the norm. As reported in a Wall Street Journal article, when speaking in Saudi Arabia, Bill Gates was asked, "What are the chances of Saudi Arabia being in the top 10 countries in the world with respect to technology?" He replied, "Well, if you are not fully utilizing half the talent in the country, you are not going to get close to the top 10." The obvious question is then, what has to happen for women to be fully and equally included in the workforce so that the world benefits from women working for the greater good?

The questions, stories, and practices in this chapter are invitations for dialogue and learning to create conditions that enable you and the women with whom you work to thrive and make a positive difference in the world.

8-1. In the Driver's Seat at Work

Thriving women put themselves in the drivers' seats of their own work lives. They set goals and do what it takes to achieve them. They seek opportunities to learn and to grow, along with opportunities for innovation, fun, and adventure. They organize their lives to balance work and rest, learning and achievement, helping others and caring for themselves. Inequalities and injustices that are roadblocks to some are stepping-stones to success for thriving women working with dignity and grace.

1. Tell me about a time when you were in the driver's seat of your work life. When was it?

   » What were your goals at the time?

   » What did you do to achieve them?

   » How did you balance work and rest?

2. Reflecting upon your work life now, what situation could benefit by you getting into the driver's seat?

   » What do you need to do to get things in balance?

   » How will you do so?

   » Who can you ask for help?

3. What tips do you have for younger women about how to live their work lives in the driver's seat?

8-2. It Pays to Include Women

Businesses around the globe are benefiting from women's participation in the workforce. Organizations that welcome women and increase gender diversity see corresponding increases in financial results, innovation, and employee satisfaction. People report enjoying work more when there are women in the workplace, appreciating that women take time to care and encourage others to be their best. Companies with women in senior management positions and on their boards of directors report higher financial returns to shareholders, illustrating that it pays to include women.

1. Tell me about some of the ways that women are actively included and made to feel welcome in your business or workplace.

   » How have you personally included women in your work?

   » How have women responded? Others?

2. In what ways has your business or workplace benefited by including women?

   » What about women in the workplace creates these benefits?

   » How do you show appreciation for the women who have contributed to these benefits?

3. If you could airdrop a team of women into any department or organization, where would you send the team?

   » Why do you think this organization could benefit from more women?

   » How would involving more women change the organization for the better?

8-3. Women at the Table of Power

The number of women in positions of formal power, having a seat at the table, is growing, and the benefits are evident. Businesses and communities make better decisions and do better with an increase of women in leadership. Women's issues are more likely to be addressed and attended to if women are at the table, often resulting in enhanced retention of women in key positions and higher levels of satisfaction among women and men throughout the organization.

1. Tell me about a woman you consider a powerful leader, past or present. Who is she?

    » What do you respect and admire about her?

    » How does she use the power of her position in a good way?

    » What can we learn from her about having a seat at the table and having a positive influence?

2. Thinking about yourself, at what table of power would you like a seat?

    » What would you do in that position of power?

    » How will you get there?

    » Who can help you along the way?

3. Imagine that you have a magic wand and when you wave it, a woman gets a seat at a table of power.

    » What woman?

    » What position of power?

    » Why did you make this choice?

8-4. Powerful Feminine Expression

Women express themselves in a wide variety of ways. Some are quietly intuitive, pausing before speaking and using few but meaningful words. Others gesture freely, dress boldly, and seem to speak in exclamation marks. Whatever their styles, women's powerful feminine expression can inspire others to action. They can use it to gather people and resources in service of a greater good.

1. What does powerful feminine expression mean to you?

   » What three or four adjectives describe it?

   » What messages did you hear as a child about being feminine? How have they helped you succeed at work?

   » What TV personalities or characters did you admire as successful feminine women? Why did you admire them?

2. Tell me about a time when you inspired others to action.

   » How did you do it?

   » How did you feel at the time?

   » If I asked the others involved, how would they describe your style of expression?

3. Bella Abzug had her hats, Hillary Clinton has her pantsuits, and Ruth Bader Ginsburg has her dissent collar. What is your favorite feminine symbol?

   » Why is it especially meaningful to you?

   » When do you show it?

   » How do people respond?

She's Crying. Now What Do I Do?

by Kathryn Britton

I was told multiple times that crying at work was career suicide. I was told it made me look weak and reinforced the stereotype that all women were weak. I tried valiantly for years not to cry.

Then I realized that I cry when I am enraged. It's not a weak response. It's such a powerful wave of emotion that I can't hold it back. Research even shows that women have shorter tear ducts than men, making it harder for them to hide the tears that well up when they are upset. So, I stopped trying to give myself a personality transplant and faced the fact that rage brings tears to my eyes.

Let's put this in a particular context. In my experience, people rarely take criticism from a person in power without some emotional reaction, especially if no argument is allowed. Here are some of the responses I've observed in my long career, many of them by men:

- *Go back to your office and put your fist through the wall.*
- *Pack up all your books and office memorabilia, carry them out to your car, and write an "I quit" letter.*
- *Go home and complain to family about how unfair your boss is.*
- *Start giving your work the slow roll, a term that means subtly doing less and less. That might mean calling in sick more often.*
- *Bad mouth your boss in the coffee room. What an unfair manager! Then subtly sabotage some of your boss's priorities.*
- *Cry in your boss's office during the feedback meeting.*

For some reason, only crying seems to be utterly taboo, though it's probably the least destructive! In fact, crying is different in another important way. It is the only response that happens right in front of managers right at the time of the feedback. It gives them a chance to see how the feedback is landing and then ask questions, either internally or out loud: Was my feedback fair? Was there another side to the story? Was there anything I overlooked? Am I undervaluing the effect that this person has on the work of the people around her? The answers to these questions might not change the feedback, but they could provide valuable insight that will help the manager work well with that person, and maybe others, in the future. People hate tears at work because they don't know what to do. So, what can you do, whether you are the person crying or the person observing?

Normalize it. Crying is just another way to express emotion, and everybody has emotions. Managers can convey this by having a box of tissues sitting on the desk. They can ask, "Would you like to finish this conversation later?" The person can decide whether the emotion will prevent effective conversation right now or can be acknowledged and then ignored. One manager left me in his office with the tissue box and returned in five minutes, as we'd agreed. Then we both turned our attention to the situation, not the tears.

Address it with curiosity. "Why do I/you feel so strongly about this?" Does the feedback seem unjust? Are there other things going on in the person's life that are interfering with performance? It helped to be able to explain that the tears meant anger and to have a chance to explain why the situation made me angry.

Once my boss told me that I just missed the top rating. When I pushed back, he said that I had excelled, but my assignment just wasn't important enough. That started a discussion about future assignments so that I could be competing on a big enough stage. Once, my manager had forgotten one of my accomplishments from early in the year. When I reminded him, he revised the feedback. Once, I learned about something I really needed to work on. It wasn't easy to hear, but my tears dried up as I saw the justice of her words.

It's my belief that every manager who learned to deal with my tears was better prepared to deal with all sorts of emotional reactions to feedback. My tears took anger that is usually hidden and made it visible. Normalizing strong emotions and facing them with curiosity helps managers bring out the best in their people.

8-5. Stepping into Equality

Stepping into equality in the workplace requires that women learn new roles, new ways of working, and new ways of relating with each other and with men. Stepping into equality puts women on a steep learning curve requiring on-the-job learning, classroom education, mentoring, coaching, and informal relationships with supportive people.

1. Tell me a story about a time when you stepped into equality and faced a huge learning curve. What was the situation?

    » What were two or three things you learned at this time?

    » How did you learn them?

    » Who else was involved? How did they support you?

2. Women stepping into equality can make a big difference by helping each other. Who was the last woman you helped to learn?

    » What did you help them learn?

    » How did you do this?

    » Tell me about your relationship.

    » How did it feel to help another woman learn to step into equality?

3. Think about all that women need to learn in order to succeed in male-privileged workplaces. What are the three most important messages you can give a woman about how to succeed while maintaining dignity and self-confidence at work?

Becoming a Team Player

By Maria Giovanna Vianello

I'm an Organizational Development professional, an executive coach, and a member of several high performing teams of women. I have beautiful relationships with my two sisters, my mother, and my mother-in-law. Even though we live far away, we can always count on each other. We celebrate our successes and ensure support dealing with failures. We seem to understand each other's needs and expectations even before requests have been raised.

Professionally, the situation started quite differently. A year ago, through a 360-degree assessment, I learned what my work team thought of me: I lacked collaboration and interest in contributing to the team objectives; I was distant from the team's positive spirit; and I had detached and poor communication. After receiving this feedback, I thought my report was a complete disaster. I felt so much shame that I thought of changing jobs and leaving the company. Asking myself what I was doing wrong increased my frustration. It did nothing to help me focus on solutions. I spent a few weeks consumed by negative thoughts about my experience with my team.

Finally, I decided to shift my attention from the 360 report to moments when I felt a part of this high-performing team, when we were cohesive and collaborative, and when all of us, including distant team members like myself, felt accepted. The following example describes our team working at its best.

During our first meeting with the new head of our division, we used the metaphor of a cake to redefine our priorities in light of his new role. The insides of the cake, with pieces of dried fruit mixed with cream, were our individual priorities. The layer of sponge cake was what kept us together. The external frosting and sugar decorations were the additional nice-to-have projects that could give us external visibility. We explained this metaphor to our new leader using a real and elaborate Italian Cassata cake that represented our courage, creativity, and positive spirit.

Discovering the good aspects of my relationship with my team was the secret ingredient to my personal growth. In the past, my good intentions to be part of the team were not clear to my colleagues, so I was perceived as detached. My lack of openness kept me from bonding. I must have looked like an isolated satellite. As soon as I started to be more open with the team, sharing my personal expectations, and consistently offering my time and resources, our relationship shifted. I began to anticipate the kind of support each team member needed, experiencing true compassion. Learning from positive experiences such as the Casata cake event, I did things that shifted others' perceptions of my behaviors and intentions.

Reading the results of my latest 360 reports a few days ago was one of my most rewarding professional experiences in twenty years. I felt my positive intentions were now clear and my impact more significant. The team was proud of my contribution, and I belong. In the new report I'm described as clearly committed to my work, passionate about the team agenda, and always willing to roll up my sleeves to support the team priorities.

I feel honored to be part of a highly focused, highly skilled, and hyper-aligned team. When we face challenging circumstances like massive organizational changes, I know we can count on each other, just as I can count on the women in my family.

8-6. CHALLENGING GENDER STEREOTYPES

Thriving women challenge gender stereotypes when they call for changes that improve the status of women at work, when they do something first that was previously prohibited for women to do, and when they speak up about oppressive norms in the workplace. While being the first to do something can be exciting, it may also take great courage to go against social norms and relational expectations.

1. Tell me about a woman you know or have heard of, whom you admire for being the first woman to do something. Who is she?

   » What did she do?

   » What gender stereotype did she challenge and change?

   » How has she inspired you?

2. Now tell me about a time when you challenged a gender stereotype. What was it?

   » What led you to challenge it? What did you do?

   » What changed because of what you did?

   » Who helped and what did they do?

   » How did it feel at the time? Afterwards?

3. What gender stereotype do you believe most needs to be changed these days? If you were to make an award for challenging this stereotype, what would you call it?

8-7. POSITIVE CONVERSATIONS ABOUT EXCLUSION

When we observe or experience gender bias, harassment, or exclusion at work, it is an opportunity to speak up. For change to occur, we need to talk to the people who exclude or harass us. Often, these are not easy conversations. When they go well, however, they can be very positive. Everyone learns, and relationships are strengthened. Keys to success in these conversations are expressing that you care enough to confront, that you value the person and your relationship, and that it is very important to be able to speak without being interrupted. In some cases, rehearsing with a supervisor or a friend can make the conversation easier.

1. Tell me about a time when you had a conversation about exclusion with someone at work. What was the situation you talked about?

   » What made it possible for you to initiate the conversation?

   » How did it go? Did you feel heard? Understood?

   » What changed as a result?

   » What did you learn from this conversation?

2. Who in your experience is an exemplary model of leadership that supports gender equality and full inclusion?

   » What does this person do that shows support for gender equality and inclusion?

   » How does this person's gender and inclusion style affect the people and performance of the organization?

⟳ A Practice: Inclusion Buddies

Inclusion is something we do together, so it is best learned and practiced together. People experience inclusion differently. This practice is a way to improve inclusive communication.

Partner Up

1. Think of a person with whom you regularly interact who is different from you in gender, race, age, ethnicity, or sexual orientation. Invite that person to be your inclusion buddy.

Agreement

2. Decide how long you want to be inclusion buddies. We suggest one month.

3. Discuss what you both mean by inclusion, and share what you each want to improve in your own behavior, for example, asking questions rather than interrupting women when they talk, or speaking truth to power about exclusion, or recognizing the valuable contributions of women of color when they speak.

4. Determine when and how you will give each other appreciative feedback for demonstrating positive inclusive communication.

Appreciative Feedback

5. Meet with your inclusion buddy and give each other appreciative feedback based on observations of each other's communication and behaviors. For example, appreciative feedback on gender inclusion might sound like this:

   » "I noticed that you spoke up about how you felt about the strategy in our meeting. I know this was something that you were working on. It really helped us to have your insight."

   » "Thank you for letting the chair know he was sidelining women's voices. I appreciated the way you spoke up."

6. As you share, deepen your learning by asking questions such as,

   » How did it feel when you spoke out?

   » How did it feel when you acted in this way?

   » How could I have supported you more?

   » What else do you want to practice to enhance your capacity for inclusive behavior?

Closing

7. When the agreed upon time is up, have one final meeting to share lessons learned and express gratitude to each other for being inclusion buddies.

Try saying this silently to everyone and everything you see for thirty days and see what happens to your own soul. 'I wish you happiness now and whatever will bring happiness to you in the future.

Joan Chittister

8-8. STRENGTHS OF INTERSECTIONALITY

Women living and working at the intersections of race and gender have greater challenges to navigate in the world of work than do their white women colleagues. They also have unique strengths and different perspectives to contribute as a result of their intersectionality. For all women, success means that they must learn and adapt to the many ways male privilege exists in the workplace. Intersectionality creates capacities to meet these challenges.

1. Tell me about intersectionality in your life.

   » What are the intersectional issues you face? Race, gender, physical ability, sexual orientation, poverty?

   » What do you do to succeed at these intersections?

   » What strengths have you discovered or developed because of your life at these intersections?

2. Tell me about an organization or institution that successfully understands and highlights the strengths of intersectionality.

   » What does it do to meet the needs of women working at the intersection of race, gender and perhaps poverty?

   » How does it ensure that women of different backgrounds are included and given opportunities to thrive?

   » How are the strengths of intersectionality brought to light and aligned with the goals of the organization?

3. Imagine a world where the intersection of gender and race is visible, needs are being met, and strengths are being celebrated. How would it be different from your world today?

8-9. Contributing to the Greater Good

Thriving women work for many reasons: to earn a living, to learn and grow, and to make positive differences in the lives of their families, communities, and the world. From villages where micro-financed businesses run by women feed entire communities, to global corporations bringing bold life-saving innovations to the world by including women at all levels, to legislative bodies where women bring family issues to the forefront, the work of thriving women benefits the greater good.

1. Tell me about your work and how it benefits others, your family, your community, or the world. What do you do?
   » What inspires you to do this work?
   » What about it gives you joy?
   » How do others benefit from your work?

2. Imagine that it is some time in the future. You are about to walk into your retirement party.
   » What do you hope people will say about you at this party?
   » How will they describe your work's contribution to the greater good?
   » What, especially, will other women thank you for?

3. Imagine that you have a large sum of money that you could donate to any cause on earth. What would it be, and why?

4. It is 2025, and we are living in a peaceful and sustainable world. What part have thriving women played in making this come about?

8-10. A Culture of Inclusion

Organizations, large and small, can be places that tend and befriend diversity in all aspects of business, rather than control it out. Organizations do this by building a culture of inclusion in which the core values of diversity, equality, and collaboration are instilled into everything people do. Organizational culture is simply "the way we do things around here." In a culture of inclusion, the ways things are done are fair and equal, with women and men working respectfully together and with leadership enacting full inclusion as a daily practice.

1. Think about the many organizations you know, large and small. Tell me about one that has an exemplary culture of inclusion. What is the organization?

   » What leads you to describe its culture as an example of inclusion?

   » How is inclusion woven into processes, structures, and culture?

   » Does the organization have unique and inclusive human resource practices? What are they?

   » How are people promoted?

   » How does leadership talk about and demonstrate the importance of inclusion?

2. Now imagine a thriving organization that has no need for diversity or inclusion programs. It is an organization where women and men collaborate with ease, where work is liberating and socially satisfying, and where people work from their strengths in alignment with each other.

   » Describe this organization to me. What is its mission? How are people recruited, developed, and promoted?

   » Tell me about leadership in this thriving organization.

Appreciative Inquiry Gender Inclusion Summit

by Tanya Cruz Teller and Marlene Ogawa

We sat in wonder, reflecting on the successfully completed Gender Inclusion Summit for Genesis Analytics that we had just facilitated. The sun was setting over our venue, the beautiful Johannesburg Country Club, a former bastion of exclusion reserved for white men only. Being there for this purpose magnified our feelings of success. We felt elevated in our work, confirmed in our Appreciative Inquiry methodology.

Our clients left feeling more hopeful and connected within and across genders, with an increased sense of awareness, a shared responsibility, and a comprehensive plan for gender inclusion. During the summit, the Appreciative Inquiry (AI) process enabled them to plan for inclusion, while at the same time giving them an experience of being included. That was the game changer.

We began the summit with appreciative interviews. Participants were invited to share stories about their personal experiences of gender inclusion. Listening to each other's stories of peak gender inclusion experiences was transformative. People reported an increased sense of empathy, as well as a feeling of being seen and heard in a new way. They experienced inclusion.

Here are some examples of the spirit of inclusion. Two peers, different in gender and race, sat huddled interviewing each other about what enabled open feedback about gender inclusion. A pair of women, different in levels and race, sat knee-to-knee interviewing each other around a specific situation where the white supervisor understood and was able to champion a situation specific to her black female staff. A rising young female sat with a male leader of the company sharing how his willingness to welcome her tears in a meeting enabled her to feel whole at work and shine thereafter. A gay male and a straight female pair connected the experience of inclusion as a gay man to the need to advocate for women's inclusion. Another pair discussed the positive impact of a male supervisor interrupting gender-based exclusion that the female staff had experienced with a client.

The interviews and discussions that followed created two big shifts. Participants described a renewed sense of themselves as positive actors in their own lives. They also felt a deeper connection to others. Telling a story and actively listening strengthened trust.

Following the appreciative interviews, we invited participants to create a picture of the gender-inclusive positive core of Genesis Analytics: the values, beliefs, ways of working, and ways of treating each other that are at the heart of its success. The trust created during the appreciative interviews fostered open discussions and vulnerability as the group went through the AI dream and design phases.

Focusing on their future together and designing in groups allowed sharing bold ideas, equalized the power in the room (and in the company), and further strengthened relationships among diverse colleagues. Everyone said they had both shared and learned. They felt heard, and they listened to understand.

We ended the Gender Inclusion Summit with a circle of personal commitments and appreciations. Here are some of their comments: "I'd like to know more about your experiences as a black woman." "I'd like to share more of my experience as a rural black woman working in this big city firm." "I want more women to know they can become mothers at Genesis." "As a man I understand now that women know best how to be supported, and I can just ask, rather than trying to fix things." Participants said they knew what degree of inclusion was possible because they had experienced it. They had a plan to create more of what they want and need.

Our client, Genesis Analytics, engaged our firm, Mandate Molefi, a consultancy specializing in culture change and leadership development, to support their diversity, equity, and inclusion journey. Genesis

Analytics is the largest economics-based consulting firm in Africa that uses analytical capabilities to improve decision-making. They work across various domains and specialize in competition and regulatory economics, financial services strategy, agriculture and agribusiness, applied behavioral economics, infrastructure, health, monitoring and evaluation (M&E) and shared value. Except for M&E, these fields have low representation of women and especially women of color and minorities. Genesis Analytics' intentional commitment to changing this is important, given their influential role on the continent.

The Gender Inclusion Summit was a part of Genesis' commitment to address race and gender. It was followed by workshops on gender inclusion for all staff that built on the internal success stories, new vocabularies, and promising practices that were generated during the AI summit.

Reflecting on the strengthened relationships, bold ideas, and increased awareness about gender inclusion, we saw that all these were achieved by discovering what is working and amplifying what is possible. We are clear how meaningful AI can be in diversity, equity, and inclusion work. Our hope is that AI will grow as a way not only to address exclusion at work, but also to help rebuild our South African society that still has much work to do to heal and rebuild relationships so we can live our dream and be the rainbow nation.

You cannot easily fit women into a structure that is already coded as male; you have to change the structure.

Mary Beard

Mothers and Daughters

by Leah Elliott, Free Range Poet

If love were uncomplicated,
where would be the flavor?
Friction is evidence of connection,
those points of contact where we stick.
Sometimes for a moment.
Sometimes for moments that extend,
stretched taffy thin till the fabric seems it may break.
That's where the light shines through,
where "me" can truly see "you."
And there the smoothed over polyps become things of beauty.
Worn smooth.
Polished.

Carrboro Really Free Market
December 2, 2017

9
WOMEN SUPPORTING WOMEN

*Women who support each other to achieve personal
hopes, dreams, and goals are the change.*

When women join together for a common cause, they build unstoppable momentum for social, economic, and political change. The 1881 National Domestic Workers' Strike brought African American women higher wages and better working conditions. The suffragette movement of the early 20th century in the US resulted in the passage of the 19th amendment, giving women the right to vote.

Similarly, around the world, Las Madres, a group of grieving mothers, gather every week in the main square of Buenos Aires to recite the names of the estimated 30,000 people detained and killed by the military dictatorship that ruled the country from 1976 to 1983. Recently, 5 million women joined hands in Kerala, India to protest the inability of women to enter the Hindu Sabiramala Temple. And, every year on March 8th, International Women's Day, millions of women worldwide protest en masse for sexual-assault justice, income equality, reproductive rights, and equal rights.

When women band together for a shared goal or purpose, they accomplish unassailable feats. In the early 1960's a coalition of women, Chicago's Jane Collective, helped women find safe abortions at a time when abortions were inaccessible, especially to poor women. The creation of this book is a shining example of women together accomplishing what none could do alone.

This empowered sisterhood aimed at common causes is a potent force for social change. Women supporting other women to achieve their personal hopes, dreams, and goals is an even more powerful force for change. Consider the female scientist who helped a younger colleague successfully apply for her first patent.

Not all women, however, experience this support from other women. All too many women go through life enduring subtle or not so subtle attacks from other women. This *mean girl* phenomenon is described as a young girl challenge, yet adult women often tell of other women blocking their promotions, undermining their ambitions, going silent at the news of their successes, and gossiping about everything from their dress to their ambitions to their morals. Dr. Rumeet Fillan and Todd Humber reported that almost 90% of 1500 female professionals surveyed in Canada reported being undermined at work, often at the hands of women they considered friends or trusted colleagues.

Perhaps this is why the training regimen of American distance runner, Shalane Flanagan, the first woman in 40 years to win the New York City Marathon, got the attention of writers. While her triumph at the age of 36 was unique, especially after years of physical setbacks, what is even more unusual is what happened to the group of female distance runners Flanagan invited to live and train with her. Dubbed the *Shalane Effect*, Flanagan's decision to invite her competitors to join her resulted in all eleven of the women making the Olympic team and achieving their own personal best times. These results are spectacular by any athletic training standard, but especially for women, who have typically trained in isolation, often burning out and not achieving their potential. Flanagan has created a blueprint for how women can be fierce competitors, and simultaneously nurture and encourage each other. There is much we can learn from Flanagan and others like her who support women to be their personal best.

The questions, stories, and practices in this chapter are invitations to dialogue about women supporting women to be their best.

9-1. Women Who Bring Out Our Best

Many of us have other women who bring out our best. They may be colleagues, teachers, mothers, grandmothers, aunts, children, or friends. They have our backs in challenging situations and share their knowledge, wisdom, and recipes at just the right time. They bring out our best by seeing our strengths before we do and by caring enough to confront us when we could do better.

1. Tell me about a woman who regularly brings out your best. What is your relationship?

    »   What does she say or do that brings out your best?

    »   How do you feel in her presence?

    »   What is the most wonderful thing she's done to help you feel good about yourself?

2. Tell me about a time when another woman recognized something good about you before you saw it yourself. What was it?

    »   What were you doing?

    »   How did she notice your goodness?

    »   What did she tell you about it?

3. Tell me about a time that you were inspired by witnessing a woman recognize and bring out another woman's best self. What was the situation?

    »   What did she do or say that inspired you?

    »   What impact did this have on the other woman?

    »   What impact did that experience have on you?

9-2. Fierce Supportive Competition

Like Shalane Flanagan, we can put aside divisiveness among competitors and instead practice, learn, and support each other so that everyone wins by achieving their personal goals. Without fear of losing power or status, we can share professional tips, intellectual property, introductions to helpful others, and our personal secrets for success.

1. Tell me about a group of women who are both competitors and supporters with you.

   » What do you do that places you in competition?

   » How do you support one another and learn together?

   » What are the benefits of this association for you and others?

   » Based on this positive experience, what would you say to a woman who complains to you about her competitor?

2. In what activity would you like to play up, interacting with women who are better than you? Why this activity?

   » Who are the women who are better at it than you are?

   » What makes interacting with them a great way to learn?

3. Now consider an activity that you are willing to play down, helping women behind you on the learning curve.

   » What do you have to offer?

   » How could you imagine doing this and having fun?

Flipping the Disney Rule

by Caroline Adams Miller

Sitting in a doctor's waiting room, I flipped through a popular magazine and stopped on a two-page spread about Kate Middleton and Meghan Markle. The two women were pictured on opposite pages, one looking to the left, the other to the right. The article focused on the alleged jealousy and anger between them. The placement of the pictures mirrors what every little girl grows up internalizing if she has been exposed to Disney fairy tales. The so-called Disney Rule says that princesses can never look in the same direction if they are shown together. Two princesses looking in the same direction is apparently problematic.

I feel like the Disney Rule governed much of my early life. My mother seemed to compete with me. She was never able to summon maternal happiness for my successes. When I was accepted to a competitive elementary school, I found her clutching my acceptance letter sobbing, "I never had these kinds of opportunities." While I developed female friendships as a young girl, it seemed that encountering mean girls was simply part of being female: suddenly being shut out of a clique that was once a safe space or being marginalized because I got a high grade or being punished for standing out noticeably.

The mean girl dynamic doesn't necessarily end when people grow up. This was driven home when the female graduate networks of Harvard and Yale in the Washington, D.C. area merged to discuss topics of mutual interest. The first one chosen was the question, "Why do women undermine other women?" The meeting coincided with the election of Donald Trump and the #MeToo and #timesup movements. As the media and women's advocacy groups focused on the long-overdue issues around sexual discrimination and unequal gender justice, it was important to the women at the meeting to address ways that women hold each other back.

Because of my troubled childhood, I learned early not to assume that the women closest to me will be in my corner. I learned to deliberately create a colony of female coaches, therapists, managers, cheerleaders, mentors, and friends who are happy for me when I succeed, challenge me when I need a push, and console me when I fall down. I also make a point of providing support for women who don't have an army behind them, and whose talent, ambition, looks, and excellence have occasionally hurt them more than helped them.

Talented women who don't have a support system may choose to go quiet, question themselves, stop believing in their dreams, and lower their sights. Instead of giving up, believing that no one will be happy for us if we achieve big goals, women need to be thoughtful about who we spend time with. I look for people that are curious and enthusiastic when I confide in them, avoiding people that respond in more negative ways.

I have consciously chosen to flip the Disney Rule. I invite you to join me. When you hear, read, or witness another woman's success, share it immediately to two social media networks. I do this twice a week with #share222 (share two women's successes to two social media networks twice a week). By sharing their accomplishments, we give women a larger platform to be discovered and honored. We stop promoting the notion that power is limited for women. We show that there's room for more than just a few powerful women.

When women support women, we can live together in harmony looking in the same direction. We can create a future filled with many princesses shining in ever-expanding rooms, all contributing their unique gifts without fear of being silenced or wounded. We can build the castles of our dreams where our daughters, granddaughters, and future generations of women will be able to pull up a chair at any table and be heard, seen, and successful.

9-3. ASKING FOR SUPPORT

We all have times when we need a helping hand. It might be something simple, such as, the name of a good realtor, or more substantial, like a letter of recommendation. It can be hard to say, "I need support," "I need someone to listen," or "I need someone to stand up for me." Often, we need support at times when we feel least deserving. It is in these moments, that we need to ask for support from people who will remind us of our goodness and help us.

1. Tell me about a time you asked for support and got it. What was the situation?

   » What did you ask for? How did you ask?

   » Who did you ask? How did they respond?

   » What did support mean to you?

2. Tell me about a time when you took a big risk to ask a woman outside of your inner circle for support and it went well.

   » What did you need at the time?

   » Who did you ask? Why them?

   » How did they respond?

   » How did you feel during this situation?

3. Make a list of three things that you need support for right now.

   » Who can you ask to help you with each item?

   » When will you talk with them and ask for their support?

4. Reflect for a moment. What ideas do you have for teaching girls that it is not only okay, but also essential to their well-being, to ask for help and support?

9-4. Learning from Role Models

One way we develop confidence to do something is to see role models doing what we want to achieve. Sometimes these role models are figures from history books, newspapers, or documentaries. Sometimes they are people close by in our families or communities. Role models speed our learning by showing us positive examples of how to live and succeed.

1. Tell me about a thriving woman role model who inspired you to take on a new challenge. Who are they? What did they do?

   » How did you find them?

   » How did observing them make you feel?

   » What did you learn?

   » How has your life been better as a result of having them as a role model?

2. Imagine sitting across from a role model and having an intimate conversation. What would you want to ask them?

   » What would say that you respect and admire about them?

   » Why are these things important to you?

3. Tell me about a time when someone told you that you are their role model. What did they say?

   » What did they learn from you?

   » How and when did they learn this from you?

   » How do you feel about being a role model?

WHAT I LEARNED FROM FIRST LADIES

by Shannon Polly

I've always been fascinated by First Ladies. I wrote my first solo show about Eleanor Roosevelt and to this day remember one of her best quotations: "You gain strength, courage and confidence by every moment in which you must stop to look fear in the face. You must do the thing you think you cannot do." I must have looked ridiculous as a 13-year-old with an old timey outfit and a wig playing Eleanor, but she was my first version of a hero.

Then came Eisenhower. I'm from Kansas and he is one of our native sons. From Abilene, Ike was a darling of the state and the country, especially during World War II. Perhaps my first act of feminist activism was writing a play about the women in his life: his mother, Ida; his wife, Mamie; and his driver/lover, Kay Summersby. I titled my play: Eisenhower and the Women Who Made Him Famous.

Ida Eisenhower was a rebel in her day. The aunt and uncle who raised her did not believe girls should be educated, and instead pushed her to memorize the Bible. When told she couldn't enroll in high school, she ran away.

Mamie Eisenhower, also a bit of a rebel, was traditionally known as one of the best dressed first ladies, but was also very thrifty, clipping coupons for the White House staff.

Perhaps the most controversial was Ike's driver who doted on him. She claims in her memoir that he tried to have an affair with her, but was too spent from the war's demands to follow through.

I performed it all around the state, for aging veterans at nursing homes and for students at various schools. But the people at the Eisenhower Museum in Abilene did not like my title. "Eisenhower did not need anyone to make him famous," they said. They refused to take the recording of my show into the library until I changed the title.

This show gave me the opportunity to meet another first lady. I was sixteen and my high school librarian, Mike Printz, was the head of the American Library Association. Barbara Bush's initiative was reading, so she sponsored an event at the White House every year. I snagged a spot performing at the Library of Congress and going to a reception at the White House, where I met the first lady herself. I was beside myself. What would I say? What would she say? Would she actually come to the performance? (She didn't. She was busy.)

As it turned out, Barbara in person was like Barbara on TV.

Down to earth. Direct. Welcoming.

She said, hello, congratulated me warmly, and sent me to the dessert table.

She was like the captain of a ship and a hostess at the same time. You knew she was running the show and she was born to do it. Being married to a president and mother of a president is no small feat. Perhaps she deserves a show called The Georges and the Woman Who Made Them Famous.

As it turns out, I did end up playing Barbara Bush in a NYC Fringe Festival musical about her son, George Dub-yah. It wasn't very flattering for her son or Barbara, I'm afraid. But it was funny.

Here's to a woman who valued sticking together and did not encourage infighting.

Here's to a woman who was a force of nature without having to be front and center.

Here's to a woman who was true to herself. White hair and all. (That's the one piece I'm not willing to follow, but I respect it.)

Thank you, Barbara. For hosting a little gal from Kansas on her first trip to the nation's capital, which has now become her home. Here's to all the First Ladies. You were models of poise and civility with a great burden to carry.

9-5. Unconditional Acceptance

We all long to be included and to feel unconditionally accepted without limitations arising from the color of our skin, our gender, sexual orientation, or accent. Feeling accepted brings contentment and fosters high performance. When we are surrounded by people who are curious, value diversity, and accept us unconditionally, we feel safe to reach for bold goals.

1. Tell me about a time when you felt completely and lovingly accepted into a group regardless of your gender, culture, color, abilities, or accent. Your unique gifts were valued and applauded.

   » What was the situation?

   » Who was with you?

   » What did they do to make you feel accepted?

   » How did this acceptance bring out your best?

2. Tell me about a time when you accepted someone of a different gender, color, status, or sexual preference in your life. What was the situation?

   » What did you do or say?

   » How did they respond?

3. Imagine it is 2025. You've just awoken from a long sleep. You look around and see people unconditionally accepting each other.

   » What are people saying and doing that is positively different?

   » Now you realize you have helped make this dream a reality. What did you do to create a world of unconditional acceptance?

9-6. Sculpting with Praise and Curiosity

Our words and actions can positively sculpt other people. When we give praise and appreciation, we tell people that we care about them, that they are valuable, and that their contributions are important. In so doing we help them do more of what they already do well, and we support their confidence to take on even bigger goals.

1. Think of a time when a woman sculpted you with praise. What did she say or do?

    » What made you feel proud of your efforts?

    » How did it feel to receive this attention?

    » What made this response meaningful for you?

    » How did it sculpt your future?

2. Recall a time when you shared good news with a woman who responded with curiosity, asking questions that helped you relive and savor the event. What was your good news?

    » Who did you tell?

    » How did she respond?

    » How did her responses add to your sense of joy and achievement?

3. Imagine someone that you would like to sculpt with praise and curiosity. Who are they?

    » What qualities or achievements would you point out?

    » What questions might you ask?

4. A newly formed women's group has invited you to help them get off to a strong start. How might you help them practice sculpting each other with praise and curiosity?

⚪ A Practice: Cultivating a Habit of Appreciation

Some people easily praise others. For others, it may take practice to notice other people's strengths and accomplishments and then to speak up about them. Use this practice to heighten your sensitivity to other people's successes and to create habits of appreciation and curiosity.

1. Pick one day of the week to focus intentionally on other women's strengths and accomplishments for fifteen minutes. It might be Monday, as you start your work week. It might be Friday as part of your week in review.

2. Begin by looking on your favorite social media sites. Who has posted an accomplishment? Immediately respond with specific appreciation. Tell others about this accomplishment.

3. Pay attention to women you encounter when you are out in public. What are they doing that helps you or other people? What do you admire about them? Tell them or send one of them a postcard or an email.

4. Watch for people whose behavior or social media posts make you think, "I wish I had done that." Twinges of envy signal of opportunities to express appreciation. Do it.

5. Speak up. End a meeting with appreciation. Invite a colleague for coffee, and tell them what you enjoy about working with them. Send an email or a card to someone congratulating them on an accomplishment.

6. At the day's end, take time to reflect. Appreciate yourself for what went well during the day. Acknowledge yourself for creating a new habit of appreciation.

9-7. Supporting and Celebrating Women

Women support and celebrate other women as best friends, as sisters, as colleagues, and as exercise buddies. From high school to college, through marriage, family, and at work, we help each other and celebrate each other's milestones – in many and varied ways.

1. Tell me about two or three women you have supported and celebrated.
   » What about them drew your attention?
   » How did those relationships come about?
   » Why and how did you support and celebrate them?

2. Tell me about a woman with whom you have a mutually supportive relationship. Who is it?
   » How do you regularly support each other?
   » How do you celebrate each other's successes?
   » What do you do to maintain the mutuality of your relationship?

3. How does supporting and celebrating other women affect you? What does it feel like?
   » How does supporting others help you grow into a better version of yourself?
   » Why is it important to you to support other women?

4. What kinds of support and celebration from other women are most meaningful to you?

A CIRCLE OF WOMEN

by Kami Guildner

And so, they gathered.

The women and the life stories that shaped each one. A mother. A sister. A friend.

A chief maker. The broken-hearted. The giver. The seer. The doer. The mistress of heart. A stranger.

And yet, there wasn't a stranger among them, for an open heart of connection gathered in that circle, welcoming all who were destined to be there. Together they brought a sense of curiosity, an energy of connection, and a knowing – like a long-forgotten song to which you somehow know all the words.

Each woman in the circle shared their story and recognized their own reflection in the stories of others. They heard stories of another's caring nature and gentle softness bounded by the fierceness of mother-bear energy. They heard stories of resilience through tough times. They felt pain, they felt strength and they celebrated the grand.

To my sister women: we are being called to gather in circle. To join in a circle of community and bold collaboration. To raise up our voices to the world – for together we are stronger.

Women in circle calls forth an ancestral knowing in our souls and releases the wisdom to lift up one another. It connects the rhythms of our lives so we can beat as one, resonating the vibrations of the feminine across the land. It gives volume to how each voice is heard and unleashes the sweet song of yin, softening the noise in our world, and inserting the gentleness of woman.

Your light, combined with her light, makes for a brighter room and a brighter world. When you open your heart to another's story, you illuminate space for her dreams to unfold and for moments of clarity to be birthed. You help give voice to the declarations of all that is possible in her life.

It is a ripple effect that gives way to a wave of fluidity and strength, changing the shape of our future world.

Today I invite you to create your own circle of women and let the magic of possibilities unfold. Invite a group of women to join you. Select a question as a starter. Then ask each woman to give voice to her story in response to the question.

- *If the whole world could hear your message, what would it be?*
- *When do you feel most alive and on fire? How do you tend to this fire?*
- *What song and music are in you waiting to come out?*
- *Tell me about a time when you stepped into twenty seconds of courage.*
- *What are you learning in your life today that is laying the foundation for your future?*

When you open your heart to the stories of another and listen – really listen – your world and her world expand. Then reach out a hand and lift her up, for together, we rise. This is the magic of circle.

9-8. Creating a Thriving Women Circle

In Okinawa, people belong to unique social structures called *moais,* groups of women or men formed in childhood with the pledge to support each other throughout life. We can all benefit by having long-running associations where we know we will be accepted just as we are, comforted in our grief, supported in our challenges, and celebrated in our successes. We can benefit from being part of thriving women circles.

1. Tell me about a time that a group of women created a warm, welcoming space for you to be supported, comforted, and challenged in positive ways.

   » Who were the women in this group?

   » How did you know them?

   » What did you all say and do to support each other?

   » What did you accomplish as a result of this sisterhood?

   » How were you positively changed as a result of being with these women?

2. Imagine an ideal circle of women for you at this stage of your life. What might bring you together?

   » Who are women that you want in your group, and why do you want them there?

   » What do you have to offer such a group?

   » Are there any women you don't know yet that you believe would be supportive group members?

   » How can you approach these women to invite them to join?

   » When will you begin?

THE GIFT OF HEARING WHAT WE NEED TO HEAR

by Diana Whitney

My mom had just died. I was overwhelmed with the funeral, her house, my brothers, the lawyer, finances, grandchildren, obituary, her friends, my own grieving.

My son suggested we go out to dinner, a nice restaurant, just the two of us. After ordering our food, he asked, "Mom what do you wish someone would say to you right now?" Tears flowed as I said what I needed to hear, what I wished someone would say to me.

He listened. He's a good listener. Then he said my words back to me. He told me what I needed to hear, "Mom, you are a great daughter. You took care of Gram really well in these last several months. You did the best you could."

"Mom, you are an incredibility generous person. By offering to pay for everyone's airfare you enabled all the grandchildren who wanted to say good-bye to Gram to see her before she died."

"And Mom, I know it is hard that Gram's lawyer is sexist and doesn't seem to trust you. You are doing the right thing with Gram's estate for the family. He doesn't know Gram's wishes better than you do. The family trusts you."

As I heard what I needed to hear, my heart opened. I felt safe and capable. I was so touched by this process that I then asked my son the same question, "What do you wish someone would say to you right now?" He told me, and when I repeated his words to him, he too cried.

"I know how much you loved Gram. Thank you for getting on the red eye and being the first family member to be here with her. Thank you for taking all the cousins out to dinner to share stories of Gram. You helped bring the family closer together." I continued until I had said all he wanted to hear. In the end, I added my appreciation for him and my gratitude for the simple yet powerfully compassionate process he shared with me.

We finished dinner with a big hug, the sweetest of all desserts.

10
MEN SUPPORTING WOMEN

The journey to freedom and social justice is not a solo journey.
Women need male allies to transform patterns of male privilege.

As a song popularized by Barbara Streisand goes, "People who need people are the luckiest people in the world." Women committed to equality must be very lucky! We need male allies. Women alone cannot transform male-privileged social patterns, policies, and laws because they entangle men as much as they do women and are about men as much as they are about women. Unequal treatment, laws limiting women's control of their lives, verbal and physical abuse are all relational acts most often imposed upon women by men wielding power. Women who are stepping into equality at work, taking back the night in their communities, and organizing to get women elected to leadership positions in government need male allies as partners in transformation.

Here are some supportive things that men we are grateful to count as allies have done for us over the years:

- Shared salary information, coaching us to ask for what we are worth
- Recommended us for jobs and consulting opportunities
- Said, "This is what I heard her say, and I agree with her."
- Volunteered to do necessary but unglamorous work
- Bragged about us to others, giving us credit for our ideas
- Invited us to meetings when others overlooked us
- Listened to accounts of inequality with empathy
- Pointed out inappropriate language to other men

It can be challenging for men to be allies. They can get pushback from other men and from groups that are not in favor of women having equal rights. They can be ostracized by members of the old boys' club. They can find themselves compelled to leave organizations and institutions that they care about when the organizations and institutions don't welcome women as equal. President Jimmy Carter left his church for precisely this reason. In June 2000, the Southern Baptist leaders voted that women should no longer serve as pastors. After a period of discernment, Carter shared his decision to break a long family tradition. In a letter he wrote in 2009, he said,

"The truth is that male religious leaders have had – and still have – an option to interpret holy teachings either to exalt or subjugate women. They have, for their own selfish ends, overwhelmingly chosen the latter. Their continuing choice provides the foundation or justification for much of the pervasive persecution and abuse of women throughout the world. This is in clear violation not just of the Universal Declaration of Human Rights but also the teachings of Jesus Christ, the Apostle Paul, Moses and the prophets, Muhammad, and founders of other great religions – all of whom have called for proper and equitable treatment of all the children of God. It is time we had the courage to challenge these views."

President Carter, along with other pattern-breaking men, including Ruth Bader Ginsburg's husband, Martin D. Ginsburg, is an exemplary role model of a male ally who journeys with women and uses his power to support the cause of equality. Thriving women welcome male allies into open dialogue about the challenges we all experience as we seek to create a shared and equal path forward.

The questions, stories, and practices in this chapter are invitations to dialogue about men supporting women to be their best.

10-1. Allies We Know and Love

There are many men who support women to be their best. They create opportunities for us and listen when we need to sort out how to work with non-supportive, perhaps even verbally abusive male colleagues. How allies support us is as varied as they are. Our fathers, brothers, sons, spouses, teachers, colleagues, and supervisors all have potential to be allies.

1. Tell me about a man whom you consider an ally.

   » Describe your relationship.

   » How did he become an ally?

   » How does he support women's equal rights?

   » What do you value and respect about him as an ally?

2. Share a story about a time when a man actively supported you to achieve an important goal or dream. What was the situation?

   » What did he do or say to support you in this situation?

   » How did you feel at the time?

   » If you were to see him today, what would you tell him about the impact he has had on you and perhaps others?

3. Reflect now on the many men in your life that you consider allies.

   » What has been the most meaningful support and help you have received from these allies?

   » What about them and the ways they support women do you most value and respect?

On Being a Male Ally in 2019

by Jordan Hackworth

I hear you. I see you. When we were young, I noticed your strength and determination. With unexpected ease and daring insight, your reflection showed me mine. Shall we walk together? I will defend you, privately and publicly, because I've seen you do the same. Ahead, with work, we can pass through trial and prejudice together. I'm sorry it took me more than a moment to notice there is so much to do. You warned me.

I can't be certain about the way forward or what to say. I don't know what is coming. But it is clear it has started. It started before we even got here. You showed me that. Thank you for giving me the pioneers and prophets who have been defining, dissecting, and dismantling the problem for so long, women who inspire and invigorate.

Here are things I'm certain about: I know to stand shoulder-to-shoulder with you. In places where you're made to feel unwelcome, in moments of struggle, and in processions of triumph. I will shout across the day and night that our voices are stronger together. We must always guard your sacred and profane spaces with strong words, unending vigilance, and, until no longer needed, swords.

Your body belongs to you. I acknowledged it with an unbreakable vow. In courts, conversations, and congresses, I will fight to make it always true. I will give my labors to widen our pathways, equally open and equally proffered. Your work is as important as mine, and must be valued as such. I'm not afraid to acknowledge that it isn't yet valued that way. Therefore, I will make political, emotional, and professional choices to end this alarming injustice.

When you are marginalized, I recoil. When you are denied a hearing, discourse suffers. This is not acceptable to me. It cannot be acceptable to me because I know what is lost when you are denied. Your world of

opportunity must be as mine, because I know what wonders you bring:
unique, unexpected, and just-in-time wonders. Until my privilege is
your privilege, I can never rest.

I vow to always remember you, even when you are not here. It
allows me to remain steadfast to this truth and always committed to our
promise. Everywhere and anytime, I will model our essential observa-
tion: together we are stronger and smarter, even as individually we are
unequivocally and separately meritorious. Thus, I will bat away forever
the ugly showers of indifference, ignorance, and intolerance. In word,
deed, and promise, I respect and value you.

The only legitimate use of privilege is to try and dismantle
the inequalities and unfairness of privilege.

Rebecca Solnit

10-2. ALLIES WHO BRING OUT OUR BEST

When asked who or what contributed to their stunning achievements in a patriarchal work environment, women often describe a male colleague, or ally, as key to their success. Allies support and encourage women to be their best and have compassion for the many challenges that women face when working and leading in male-dominant environments. They are willing to call out other men who display inappropriate language or actions.

1. Tell me about a male colleague, coach, or supervisor who brings out your best at work. Who is he?

   » What is your relationship?

   » How does he challenge you to stretch and achieve in ways you didn't think you could?

   » How does he support your initiative and leadership?

   » How has he made a positive difference in your life? Who are you because of him?

2. Tell me about a male ally who values and promotes your thoughts and ideas. Who is he?

   » How does he promote respect for your ideas?

   » How does he create opportunities for you to share your thoughts and ideas with a wider audience?

   » How does he encourage others to consider your ideas?

3. Imagine you are invited to a conference to speak about men supporting women to be their best. What would you say about why women need male allies?

   » What would you tell women to do to befriend allies?

   » What would you tell men about being a good ally?

10-3. THE SURPRISE OF SUPPORT

Every once in a while, we experience what a man does as surprisingly supportive. We do not expect it, may not have thought it was in the cards, or that he had it in him. But then it happens. He does something that is just what we need at the time, something unquestionably supportive. It may be as seemingly small as asking another man not to interrupt us or as large as taking on some of our work so that we could be free to attend a big meeting.

1. Tell me about a time when you were positively surprised by a man's supportive action. What was it?

    »   What were you doing when it happened?

    »   What did they say was their reason for doing it?

    »   How did you react? How did you feel at the time?

2. Imagine a calendar of weekly surprises of support with 52 suggestions for ways that male allies can support women. What four or five specific acts of support would you want on this calendar?

3. Imagine that there is a network of supportive men in your community who frequently surprise women with help. What kinds of things do they do?

    »   How does the media recognize and report these surprises?

    »   What are the women in your community saying about this?

    »   What three wishes do you have for this network?

10-4. Allies Who See Us

We all want to be seen, heard, and accepted for who we are at our best as well as when we are on a messy learning curve. We want to be able to tell our stories, share our ideas, and even think out loud without being interrupted or talked over. When a male ally takes time to listen to us and witness our becoming, we feel seen and validated.

1. Reflect upon a time in your life when you felt seen and accepted by a male ally. Tell me about it.

   » What was going on in your life at the time?

   » How did your ally show that he accepted you?

   » How did being seen and accepted energize or inspire you?

   » What did you go on to do and accomplish as a result?

2. Tell me about a male ally who has been by your side during a challenging time of your life. What was the situation?

   » How did his presence help you face your challenge?

   » What did he say or do that was meaningful to you?

3. Imagine that you are speaking to a group of college men about how to see and accept women in their classes. What would you tell them?

   » What tips would you give them to be good listeners?

   » How would you tell them to express understanding and acceptance of the women in their classes?

   » What story would you tell from your own experience to show why this is so important?

How I Became an Ally of Women

by Charles P. Gibbs

When I imagine the world that I'd like to live in, I see women leading the way. I see men, beginning with myself, supporting their leadership. It's a wildly inclusive world, more nurturing, more collaborative, more whole. It's a world that allows each individual to thrive and the human community to live in sustainable harmony with the whole Earth community.

I believe this transformation is possible because I've seen it happen. In 1985, I was beginning my divinity school field education placement expecting the rector, Bill Rankin, to be my supervisor. Imagine my surprise that Bill had assigned his associate, Kitty Lehman, to be my supervisor. I didn't know Kitty at all, and I resented what felt like a demotion before I'd even begun my work.

It didn't take long for me to realize what a gift it was to learn from Kitty, one of the pioneering generation of women priests in the Episcopal Church. Her father was a priest, so her roots in the church were deep. She raised consciousness, mine included, about women's gifts for ministry and the church's shameful history in discounting those gifts. She helped me imagine a transformed future.

I learned about a small group of women clergy that met for several hours before the formal beginning of the clergy conference. They met to create a circle of supportive solidarity, given the overwhelmingly male culture of the clergy. Many people were still profoundly opposed to ordaining women. Many congregations wouldn't hire a woman priest, and many congregants, including women, refused to receive communion from a woman priest.

Nowadays, female priests are often more sought after than male priests because they tend to focus more on building the congregations than on advancing their careers. Now there are many women bishops.

But back then, the path forward was exceedingly difficult for the early pioneers. The expectations of priests were grounded in male norms. Often this meant that the early women priests had to conform to male norms. In time, it would be precisely because women priests modeled female norms that they would come to be in such demand. But in those challenging early days, the hoped-for future seemed impossibly distant.

So, I began my ordained ministry learning from an exceptional woman priest and feeling I had much more in common with the inclusive spirit of the women priests I knew. That spirit included women and men, racial and ethnic minorities, gays and lesbians. From this perspective, it was a great joy to see the growing ranks of women clergy with each passing year. Over time, they went from a beleaguered minority to half or more of the clergy population, and the day came when they no longer felt the need to have a women's pre-conference gathering.

As the number of women grew, the whole culture of clergy conferences shifted. While competition was not eliminated, there was a much stronger spirit of mutual support. While the church hierarchy was not eliminated, it was made significantly more horizontal and inclusive. Those previously relegated to the margins were welcomed to a more collegial center. There was less drinking. Sexually-charged jokes and behavior became unacceptable. Women's issues became issues for the whole community. Because of that, the community became more whole.

The privilege of having witnessed and participated in the transformation of the clergy culture of the diocese is the foundation of my belief that women's leadership is central to a positive future for humanity. I commit to doing all I can to support that leadership. I cherish this commitment because it provides me a path to begin to repay the debt that I owe to all the remarkable women who have taught and supported me for the sixty plus years I've been on Earth.

10-5. Allies Calling Out Injustice

One of the most powerful actions an ally can take on behalf of women is to call out another man for inappropriate comments and actions. This takes self-confidence and clarity about values in relation to women. Arguing about right and wrong is generally not effective. When an ally expresses his values along with his discomfort about an inappropriate comment or action of another man, he opens a door for transformation.

1. Tell me about an ally who has taken a risk and called out another man. What was the impropriety or injustice?

   » How was the ally involved?

   » Were you involved? If so how?

   » What did the ally say or do? How did the other man respond?

   » What positive impact did this act have on the situation and the people involved?

   » How did it make a long-term positive difference?

2. Suppose a group of male allies were to gather to discuss ways to call out injustice effectively where you work. Who would you want invited?

   » What values would you want them to uphold about the way women are treated in the workplace?

   » What injustices would you want them to call out?

   » How would you appreciate them for calling out injustice?

10-6. Allies at Home

Many of us are fortunate to have an ally who supports and encourages us at home. He may be a partner, a friend, or a family member who treats what we do as just as important as what he does, whether it be paid work, volunteer work, or homemaking. Some allies take a fair share of childcare and housework, freeing up energy and time for us to excel at whatever we have chosen to do.

1. Think about the remarkable men in your life as friends or family members. Who comes to mind as an ally?

    » Tell me about your relationship.

    » How did he come to be an ally?

    » What does he do and say that is supportive?

    » What have you been able to do because of him?

2. What one thing, in your home life now, do you wish you had an ally's help to do?

3. If you were to teach a class of men to be allies for women at home, what would you teach?

    » What would be your three or four key messages about how to be an effective ally at home?

    » How would you teach them? What would they do?

    » How would they demonstrate their readiness to be allies?

10-7. Financial Allies

Developing financial savvy, like learning another language, is much easier with help from a native speaker. For many women, earning, saving, and having money is a relatively new phenomenon complete with choices such as how much money to ask for, what and when to save, and whether to make more money or work less. Male allies who are facile with money and at ease talking about it can help us learn about money and how to manage it successfully.

1. Tell me about someone you consider a financial ally. Who is it? What is your relationship?

   » How have they helped you make good financial decisions?

   » What helpful information and advice have they given you?

   » How do they balance giving you their opinions with support for your financial independence?

   » What impact have they had on your way of thinking about money? Your financial success?

2. Tell me about financial information you would like to understand or financial capabilities you would like to develop. What are they? Why are these things important to you?

   » Who do you know who can help you obtain this information or learn these capabilities?

   » How will you approach them and ask for help?

10-8. The Courage to Ask for Support

It can take courage to ask a male ally for support because we don't know what they will say! Having the courage to ask an ally for help can make a positive difference at times when a team is not listening to your point of view, when you call out injustice and nothing changes, when you need help deciding how much to ask for when accepting a new job, or when you suggest a way forward that strengthens relationships and are called "touchy feely."

1. Tell me about a time when you had the courage and asked an ally for support, and you got it. What was the situation?

   » Why did you believe you needed help in this situation?

   » What did you ask for? What happened as a result?

   » How did you feel at the time?

2. Think about something in your life right now that you need help from a male ally to change. What specific help do you need?

   » Why is this important to you? To others in your community or organization? To the world?

   » Who in your circle of male friends, family, and colleagues might be willing to help you in this situation?

   » How and when will you approach them with your request?

   » What will be the benefits for you and for other women when this occurs?

10-9. An Army of Allies

The world needs more men supporting equal rights and fewer men who fight to keep the old ways in place. For this to happen, men have to go through their own experiences of letting go, perhaps grieving the old ways that may have benefited them, and taking on bold experiments to practice being allies. Imagine a global army of empowered and skilled allies dedicated to supporting and following women as they lead the way to a better world.

1. Be creative and describe how the world will be positively different with this army of allies. Where will we see them?

   » How will we recognize them?

   » What will be their terms of engagement?

   » What will they be doing and saying?

2. Picture ways that women can show up differently now because of the army of allies.

   » What can they do that they could not do before?

   » How will their lives be easier?

3. Now that you've imagined the army of allies, tell me about it. How are members recruited?

   » What are the core courses for training the army of allies?

   » Who do you see leading this army of allies?

4. It is graduation day for the first class of the army of allies. You are giving the commencement speech.

   » What do you tell them about the importance of their work?

   » What vision for the future do you share with them?

Ways Men Can Support Women's Leadership

by Charles P. Gibbs

I want to acknowledge these are one man's ideas. I know there are many men who are committed allies of women whose ideas would immeasurably enrich what I offer. I'm also aware that ultimately, women are the ones who have the right to determine what support from an ally would be welcome. I hope these ideas serve as an open door for conversations that bear abundant fruit.

First, men, don't assume you know what sort of support might be helpful to a particular woman or to women in general. Ask. Then honor what you hear by offering specific, tangible support.

Second, have the humility to seek out, learn from and acknowledge the wisdom of the women around you. You might seek out a wise woman to be a mentor for your growth in understanding the feminine in leadership. There are so many all around us hiding in plain sight. Seek out more books written by and for women. Seek out movies that focus on women, their lives, leadership, and modes of being. Be prepared to discover how challenging it is to find those books and movies. Be unguarded, open, and willing to grow.

Third, cultivate a commitment to gender balance and let that guide your decisions. If you're in a position of power, use your power to ensure that women have a place at the table and public power, their voices heard.

Here's a personal example. I was often asked to give talks and/or speak on panels for a particular organization whose charter included a core principle of equitable participation of women and men. When invited to speak, I made it a practice to ask who else would be speaking. If the line-up, including me, didn't reflect equitable participation of women and men, I politely declined the invitation to make room for more women. Sometimes my response evoked, "We're sorry you won't be able to join us." More often, it evoked, "Please hold that date while we work to add women to the group of speakers."

Fourth, when women offer good ideas, support them. I don't suppose there is a woman who hasn't had the experience of offering an idea in a meeting and having it ignored. Later, when the same idea is offered by a man, it is universally acknowledged to be insightful, even brilliant. In meetings, do your best not to let that happen. Speak up. Acknowledge and value women's contributions. If you happen to be the man who echoes a woman's ignored contribution, say "Thanks, but the credit belongs to our colleague who expressed this earlier; I was only echoing her good idea."

Fifth, support the creation of spaces created and normed by women. These spaces can create critical yeast that over time helps transform the larger community and culture. At the very least, men have the responsibility to ensure that spaces are safe for women. Sexual harassment or abuse should never be acceptable. There need to be clear guidelines for appropriate behavior with education to help all members of the community live by those guidelines. There needs to be a clear and safe process for complaints to be dealt with in ways that doesn't re-victimize women.

Finally, we men need to step back from places of prominence to create open spaces for women to move into and lead. This is not to say that men's leadership is bad or unneeded, though many of the gravest challenges facing us today can be attributed to the domination-based, individualistic leadership men have practiced. Instead, it is to say that we desperately need the more cooperative, community-centered leadership that women can offer if given the opportunity.

Men, we need to learn new ways of leading from women. So, in appropriate humility, take a step back to create space and opportunity for women to step forward. Then be prepared to support them. It will change our lives for the better. It will change our world for the better.

A Daughter's Wish

by Daniel Richardsson

My daughter Indira turned 4 last week.
It was a great birthday for her and for all of us.

Two months ago, she shared a wish with me, "Dad I would like to play with all of you, Mom and Magnus, Lucia, Lilly, you, and the cat, all at the same time."

So, I decided to tell Emma, my ex, in a humble way, about our daughter Indira's wish. I suggested that maybe we could arrange something for her 4th birthday.

Last Saturday Emma came to my apartment with Lilly, Lucia, Magnus, Grandma Gisela, and a colleague from India. I had not talked with Gisela for over 3 years. My mother Anne-Maria was also there, so my daughter had both grandmothers there for her birthday wish.

It was such a nice healing experience. Emma and I even hugged as she left after the birthday cake.

I am touched, I have been praying for this to happen for years.

11
CREATING THRIVING RELATIONSHIPS

Thriving relationships are the social milieu needed to
empower women and foster a thriving world.

Patriarchal social norms, like clothing we have outgrown, constrain and limit our expression, flexibility and relational potentials in all arenas of life. In no area, however, are the constraints and limitations of male-privileged norms and expectations as intense as they are with relationships among women and men. Ancient Greek philosopher Aristotle articulated the core assumption of patriarchy, "the male is by nature superior, and the female inferior...the one rules, and the other is ruled." This assumption has shaped the relationships and identities of women and men for thousands of years. It lives on today in religious doctrines, debates on women's health care, and laws that govern our day-to-day lives. The idea of inequality separates, polarizes, and leaves us wondering how might we join together in mutual respect and harmony.

As we endeavor to create a thriving world, we seek to fashion coherence and cohesion by understanding the nature of relational patterns, not by changing people. For it is within relationships, from personal to public, that we live, find meaning, and become. It is within relationships that social norms and expectations limit us or liberate us. It is within relationships that we become our best and inspire a better world for generations to come.

As women have advanced, tension has increased in relationships among women and men. This tension has sent us alone and together in search of new ways of living and loving that are free of gender definitions and constraints. Patriarchal expectations have become toxic for men as well as women. They are harming men's physical health and emotional well-being. This does not excuse decades of violence and daily transgressions against women. It is a reminder that women and men share an obsolete social narrative, one that none of us created, that all of us keep going, and that together we must change.

What then, we wonder, gives life to thriving relationships? To relationships defined more by flexibility than by fixed gender roles? To relationships infused more with stories of complementary strengths and coordinated action than with power and patriarchy? To relationships that empower thriving women and foster a thriving world?

The questions, stories, and practices in this chapter are invitations to join with others in dialogue, to create and celebrate thriving relationships.

We have to be educated by the other. My heart cannot be educated by myself. It can only come out of a relationship with others. And if we accept being educated by others, to let them explain to us what happens to them, and to let yourself be immersed in their world so that they can get into our world, then you begin to share something very deep. You will never be the person in front of you, but you will have created what we call communion.

Xavier Le Pichon in conversation with Krista Tippett

11-1. THRIVING RELATIONSHIPS

Thriving relationships are fertile ground for us to continuously learn and develop in ways that contribute to a better world. They emerge as we care for each other and interact based on our highest values, choices, and personal orientations rather than historical social norms and patriarchal expectations. Thriving relationships are creative, collaborative containers for us to succeed at goals we select, to become the best versions of ourselves, and with others to be a force for social transformation.

1. Recall a thriving relationship in your life, perhaps an intimate relationship, a work team, or a friendship. Who are you with?

    » Tell me about a time when this relationship supported your success and helped you learn and grow.

    » What about the relationship enabled your learning?

    » What two or three adjectives best describe this relationship?

    » How have you and others nurtured this precious thriving relationship?

2. In your experience, what are the core values and norms of thriving relationships? What makes them work?

    » How do people engage with each other within and beyond the relationship?

    » How do people handle conflicts and differences?

    » How does the relationship grow and change over time?

3. Tell me about a time when you transformed a traditional relationship into a thriving relationship. Who were you with?

    » How did you do this?

    » What made this worthwhile?

WHEN RELATIONSHIPS THRIVE

by Mary and Ken Gergen

Individuals cannot be separated from the relationships of which they are a part. As constructionists, we like to talk about creating the "we" – a living being composed of "me"s but not reducible to independent selves. Thus, as the two of us have come to see it, if our relationship thrives, our well-being will prevail. But we also find that we must continuously ask ourselves, "How can we help our relationship to flourish?" So, join us as we reflect for a moment on a simple slice of daily life:

> *It was a dark and windy Tuesday night. We had just arrived home, and as we wended down our long driveway, Mary recalled that if our recycling was to be picked up early the next morning, it would be necessary to push our large recycling container back down the driveway tonight. We knew it was packed full, not only with bottles and piles of newspapers and junk mail, but with flattened cardboard boxes weighted by a recent rain. Ken said that he didn't want to do this now, not only because it was late and the night was cold and dark, but also because it is hard to see down the long drive. Mary responded that she didn't really mind and got out of the car to fetch the container. When she turned around and started to push the container up the drive, she saw that Ken had pulled the car around so the lights illuminated the drive far ahead. Mary laughed, and was very thankful to see the lights – so much better than stumbling in the dark. She finished her task and returned down the lighted drive. Ken put the car away, and they went inside the house together in a humorous mood.*

> *The story is mundane, but as we see it, the fundamental nutrient to a flourishing relationship is found in the small, almost unnoticed, details.*

As we thought about it, there are several moments in this story with important implication for how our relationship works.

Harmonizing actions: *The most obvious details in this story are found in the way the actions are coordinated: Ken doesn't wish to take on the task, so Mary does, and as Mary sets out, Ken lights her way. Each action nicely complements what has preceded it. Harmonizing actions depend importantly on a second factor, sharing goals.*

Sharing goals: *Important to harmony is singing the same song. In this story, we have both agreed on the importance of recycling. This kind of sharing depends a lot on a history of conversations together. In general, we also try to avoid having separate and competing goals; we find it alienating to bargain about "who gets what." We don't want to compromise.*

Respecting differences: *Even though we enjoy our similarities, we also try to appreciate our differences – in needs, wants, skills, and so on. It was important that when Ken didn't feel like making the trek up the dark drive, Mary didn't criticize or cajole him. It is this kind of respect that also allows us to move beyond the stereotypes of what males and females "should be."*

Rewarding relational success: *It is not incidental that we entered the house in a humorous mood. Symbolically, we were patting ourselves on the back for how smoothly and caringly we had achieved our goal. One might say we were giving kudos to this living being we call 'WE'. When the 'We' is thriving, all is well.*

11-2. RELATIONAL ROLE MODELS

There are people thriving together in the news, in the movies, writing songs, winning Nobel Prizes, and perhaps even in your own family and community. They are people, women and men, same sex couples, family members, or colleagues, who succeed by visibly sharing power and responsibilities. They collaborate and have fun doing life together. Much can be learned from them as role models.

1. Tell me about a couple, a friendship, or a partnership that is an exemplary relational role model. Who are they?

   » What is it that makes them a relational role model?

   » If I were to watch them in action, what would I see?

   » How do they show each other respect and appreciation?

   » What have you learned about relational success from them?

2. With whom do you have the most pattern-breaking relationship?

   » How does this relationship reflect your values and preferences?

   » How do you keep your relationship strong?

   » How do you share power? Responsibilities?

   » How do you have fun together?

   » What can others learn about thriving relationships by watching your relationship in action?

11-3. Negotiating Our Way Together

Thriving relationships emerge as we communicate with each other and negotiate our way together. They grow from conversations about what matters to us, about what social norms we value and want to live by, about shared goals and dreams, and about what we must disrupt to be our best. We negotiate our way together as we communicate, share decision-making, and joyfully experiment with new ways of being and thriving.

1. Tell me about a relationship that is important to you. Who else is involved? How did the relationship begin?

    » How did you get to know each other's values, goals, and life preferences?

    » Tell me about a time when you successfully negotiated your way together.

    » What social norms have you cast off or disrupted for this relationship to thrive?

2. Tell me about a relationship you have with someone very different from you. Who is the other person? How are you different?

    » How do you honor your different strengths, changing needs, and ways of being?

    » How do you talk about conflict and feelings of injustice?

    » What have you learned from this relationship that has helped you have successful relationships?

3. Imagine, you are selected to lead an innovative team of people from across the world. What is the first thing you will say or do to help team members negotiate their way together?

    » What activities and conversations will you invite them into?

    » How will you celebrate advances you make together?

Un-gendering Couple's Collaboration

by Saliha Bava & Mark Greene

We're a couple that co-writes and co-presents on relational practices. One conclusion we've reached? Gender roles are an impediment to any working partnership.

We both work in what might be called the social realms of everyday living. Mark writes and speaks about remaking manhood and Saliha consults, teaches about, and practices couples and family therapy. So, the very nature of our work is present in our lived experience every day, both personally and professionally.

As a white male, Mark is aware that his unearned privilege in the world allows him opportunities and access that others continue to be denied. Even clearer to Mark is the narrow and limiting box privilege puts him in creatively. White male privilege requires a strictly enforced performance that revolves around certainty and dominance. This traditional performance of manhood drastically limits creative options. To do truly dynamic, creative work, unearned gender-based privilege must be eliminated, allowing us to listen to, adopt, and be inspired by new ideas emerging from generative spaces of uncertainty.

As an Indian brown woman living in New York City, Saliha is conscious of how her identity is fluid and performative, as she traverses across contexts. She calls this one's hyperlinked identity, since what one is, is not who one is. Rather, who we are is constantly being redefined and negotiated in the turn-by-turn of relating. A sense of fairness is created from within these relational negotiations, depending on the context.

From the marriage of our passions for social change, we have co-developed these practices for success in our personal and professional life of collaboration:

Appreciation. *As simple a gesture as "Thanks for cleaning the* *kitchen counter"* or *"Thanks for working so hard for our family,"* makes the difference between being seen or not seen for the everyday mundane tasks we do within our relational spaces.

Seek permission. *"Hey, I want to change topics. OK?"* Not only when we are in the midst of a challenging conversation, but in everyday ordinary interactions, we seek permission of the other, thereby acknowledging the equality that co-creation requires.

Deep curious listening. *"How do you want me to listen?"* is a question we might ask the other, especially when we are stuck or the other appears stressed. We do this even without asking the other, by suspending our urge to jump in or interrupt, especially when we are co-constructing a project.

Build not block. To avoid blocking, we actively seek to build on each other's ideas. Thus, when we co-write, we each write a bit and give it to the other, who then relates to the new content by building upon it and writing into the paper.

Idea wall. We have a giant whiteboard which serves as a visual collaboration space and a placeholder for ideas, symbols, and drawings that provides clarity in co-creation.

Attend to our relational space. All of the above practices help us focus on our relational space, the relationship that we are creating through our everyday interactions and conversations. Often, we pause and ask, *"What are we creating by speaking in this way?"* drawing our collective attention to our process rather than the project on hand. We pause and consider together what we are creating in our relational context.

Collaboration and co-creation are an extension of playful and dynamic relating. As a couple that seeks to collaborate, our first task has been to create a space in which we can relate, iterate, and co-create, unencumbered by the limitations of unearned and earned status or privilege.

11-4. Doing What We Each Enjoy

In thriving relationships, we do what we each enjoy, and we share the load – the unpaid and non-promotable work as well as the income and promotion-earning work. By aligning interests, strengths, and work, performance increases, we get more done together, we feel supported, and we have more fun. Doing what we each enjoy makes life easier and work more effective.

1. Recall a time when you and others decided to work by aligning your interests and your strengths. What was the situation?

    »   What tasks or jobs did you do and why?

    »   What did others choose to do that surprised you?

    »   What results did the alignment of your strengths generate?

    »   What did you enjoy in this situation?

2. Share a story about a time when you and others shared work, perhaps in your family or at work or in your church or in your community. What work did you share?

    »   How did the decision to share this work come about?

    »   What benefits did you and others gain for sharing work?

    »   How did you and others make sharing work fun?

3. Imagine an organization wanting to shift the balance of unpaid and non-promotable work from women to share it equitably with men.

    »   What two or three tasks would you want shared?

    »   Describe how this new work-sharing program might operate.

    »   How would sharing unpaid work improve relationships among women and men at work?

➲ Practices: Experiments for Un-Gendering at Home

The following practices are experiments to stimulate dialogue and actionable steps toward relational responsibility, equality, and a healthier and happier home. Have fun with them.

Flip the Script: Have everyone in your household pick a chore that they consider outside of their traditional gender identity and do it for a week.

Share the Fun: Engage in an activity deemed traditionally masculine (boxing) or traditionally feminine (pedicure) together.

Set the Stage: When the need for a conversation about a stressful or emotional situation arises, begin by asking your partner "How would you like me to participate in the conversation?"

Feelings Matter: Express a full range of feelings; select and playfully exaggerate feelings that are generally considered masculine and feminine.

Free Range Children: Give children space and activities to discover what interests them, what they like, and what they are good at without being gender-identified. Let them wear what they wish.

The Money Game: Pay bills together, and talk about shared finances. Ensure that both parties have access to financial accounts and are financially empowered.

Divide and Conquer Together: Create a master list of shared responsibilities: the household chores, childcare chores if you have children, and social life tasks. Divide tasks based on personal preferences and what feels equal to you both.

Share a Social Life: Share responsibilities to organize social events with friends, vacations, and dates for the two of you as well as responsibilities for holiday shopping and celebrations.

11-5. Celebrating Relational Success

Successful couples, partnerships, and friendships focus more on shared actions than on individual actions. They cultivate rich vocabularies of us, we, and our, using words like "in sync," "in alignment," and "in harmony." They note and celebrate relational successes. They celebrate how they do things as well as what they've done. When we move from being individual parts of a relationship to being caretakers of a mutually cherished relationship, there is much to celebrate.

1. Tell me about a time when you and a partner, a colleague, or a friend celebrated your relationship, the way you do things together, or a time you had an important conversation.

   » With whom did you celebrate this relational success? What did you celebrate?

   » What contributed to this relational success?

   » How did you celebrate? Who else celebrated with you?

   » How does this relationship bring out your best?

2. When you think of celebrating relational successes, how is it different from celebrating an individual's successes?

   » What do you celebrate?

   » What does relational success mean to you?

   » What metaphor best explains relational success?

3. Think about a department or team that you have been part of that deserves an award for relational success. What group is it?

   » In what ways is this group or team relationally focused?

   » If you were to give its members an award for relational success, what would it be for?

   » What would you call the award?

☙ A PRACTICE: RELATIONAL HARMONY VIA DIALOGUE

One way to shift gender narratives from patriarchal to thriving is to shift conversations from talking about what he is or is not doing or what she is or is not doing to talk instead about who we are and what we are doing. Thriving relationships are characterized by relational harmony – times when the ways we are together make sense, are meaningful, and generate a resonance uniquely their own.

To explore and enhance relational harmony, take turns sharing your answers to some or all of the questions below. Consciously create relational harmony as you share your answers by chanting, "we agree, we agree" when you do; and by chanting "we are different, oh yea, we are different, oh yea" when you disagree. Laugh a lot when you both agree and when you differ. Make both a fun way to be.

1. We are most in harmony when we...

2. We are in loud and boisterous harmony when we...

3. We are in soft and subtle harmony when we...

4. The ways we get back in harmony after being apart are...

5. Ways we invite each other into harmony are...

6. Things we do best when we are in harmony are....

7. When we are in harmony people seem to....

After everyone has shared answers to the questions, discuss this question: How has our relationship shifted as we shared answers and talked about relational harmony?

Great resourcefulness lies within us and between us…
if we are willing to trust ourselves and each other.

Carrie Newcomer and Parker J. Palmer

11-6. Compassionate Communities

Compassionate communities welcome everyone. They provide a safe place of belonging. At their best, they are intergenerational, kind-hearted, and inclusive of all people. This is especially important, and too often missing, for those with non-traditional gender orientations and those who are elderly or differently abled. Whatever the purpose of the community, it is a safe space for people to talk, listen, laugh, cry, teach, and learn together.

1. Tell me about a compassionate community that you have been part of. Who are its members?

    » How do they show up and participate?

    » What do you value about being part of this community?

    » How does this community bring out your best?

    » What do you do to care for and nurture this community?

2. Recall a time when you belonged to a community that included people quite different from you. What was the community? What did you do together?

    » How did differences among the people enhance the situation and create conditions for thriving?

    » What did you value about being part of this community?

    » Who or what made it a meaningful affiliation for you?

    » What made it creative and fun?

3. If you were to create a version of your compassionate community somewhere new where it does not yet exist but is needed, where would this be? Why?

    » How would you do this?

    » Who would you ask to help you?

11-7. Sharing Power and Leadership

Women and men are sharing power and sharing leadership for social change in their cities, towns, and villages, and in businesses around the world. As mayors, government officials, health care providers, community organizers, and leaders, they are making a positive difference in the lives of girls and women in their communities. They are changing laws, rewriting policies, and ensuring community safety, all with women's needs and gender equality in mind.

1. Tell me about women and men who share leadership in your community or organization.

   » How does their work together make a difference?

   » With whom do they work to make this possible?

   » What do you respect and admire about how they share power and share leadership?

2. Now think about a successful collaboration among women and men fostered by women in your community. Who is involved? What are they doing?

   » How did they get started?

   » Why have they been so successful?

   » What positive impacts have they had?

3. Imagine a training program to learn about sharing power and leadership. You get to spend a month with a city, town, or business leader who shares power and leadership.

   » With whom would you want to learn about sharing power?

   » What do you respect about their collaboration?

   » What collaborative project would you want to do? With whom? Why?

11-8. CHANGING LAWS, CHANGING LIVES

Laws and policies are an essential part of governance. Intended to keep us safe, to provide security, and to care for those unable to care for themselves, they influence our lives and our relationships. As laws change, so too do the possibilities of our lives. Many of us have experienced changes in laws that affect our relational identities, our finances, our right to vote, and our body choices. It's our job to ensure that our laws reflect our deepest values.

1. Tell me about a change in a law that has affected you and people you care about. What law is it?

    » How has it affected your life? The lives of other people?

    » Who and what was involved in changing this law?

2. What law currently enables you to be your best self? Why is it important?

    » What positive impacts is it having in your life?

    » What needs to change in order for you and others to freely be your best selves?

3. Most of us live according to a personal code of conduct. Tell me about yours. What three to four principles do you live by?

    » What happens when you break your own code of conduct?

    » How do you get yourself back on course?

4. What is your most hopeful dream for your country? What laws need to change to realize this dream?

    » What new laws are needed?

    » What laws need to be dismantled? Why?

    » If you were given the opportunity to change the laws of the land, how would you go about doing it?

    » Who would you involve? How?

11-9. "Ourstory"

The news is out: schools and universities around the world are closing their history departments. They will teach *ourstory* instead. These innovative educators are taking a big leap forward. Both history and herstory will be part of the *ourstory* curriculum; neither will dominate, be privileged, or be taught as more correct than the other. Students will read stories of the past about heroic and courageous men. They will also read stories of powerful and influential women. The new *ourstory* curriculum, telling of people who together raised families, founded communities, and led us to a sustainable world, will be launched this year in over 40 countries.

1. You are on the curriculum design committee. Your first job is to identify stories of people who have together made a positive difference in the world.

   » Who do you propose be included? Why? Who else?

   » Where would you send a team of students to do research to identify more ourstories? What communities, what countries, what organizations?

2. The new curriculum will include our origin story, not the origin of men, but the origin of people together setting a course to a sustainable world. Who would you include in our origin story?

3. The new curriculum is ready. As you review it you realize that your story is part of ourstory. Tell me about it.

   » With whom have you collaborated and positively contributed to social justice? What did you do?

   » With whom have you partnered to create a sustainable world that works for all? What did you do together?

EACH OF US WILL DIE ONE DAY

by Charles Gibbs

Each of us will die one day –
it doesn't matter.

More important is to practice living.
Still all that does not serve
our truest becoming.

Listen to the music of the universe
inviting us to begin
the dance that is ours alone.

The Beloved has been waiting
from before time
for our first step
for our next step.

No matter our age,
our life is new in this moment –
Let us dance.

12
LIVING LIFE AS A WORK OF ART

A life well lived is a work of art leaving the world a better place.

One might say, "Who has time for play and creativity?" We respond, "Who does not?" Women throughout time have sung and told stories as they worked, transforming life from drudgery to artistry. They have made pottery cups and bowls that are both functional and beautiful, and they have supported themselves and their families by making and selling handicrafts. A life well lived is a life of artistry, no matter what form the art takes. Of course, Martha Graham, Georgia O'Keefe, Louise Nevelson, Billie Holiday, Joan Baez, Madonna, dancers, painters, and singers come to mind as women living lives of artistry. Consider also the lives of Rosa Parks, Gloria Steinem, Eleanor Roosevelt, Joan of Arc, Margaret Mead, Rachel Carson, and Malala Yousafzai. They disrupted social norms to advance the causes of their hearts, leaving the world better because of their actions. They lived life as a work of art.

Artists tend to live and work on the edges of society. Their work is to bend and break boundaries, to create new expressions of beauty, and to stimulate awe and wonder about the extraordinary meaning of ordinary life. A painter, for example, who identifies her work as realism invites dialogue about the meaning of what is real. Does her sky look real? Upon hearing the critique that his paintings were not real, Picasso wrapped the edges of a painting with a real piece of rope and asked, "Is that real enough?" In doing so, he is said to have created the first collage! In life as in art, conversations about what is real and what is ideal lead to innovation and social transformation.

Artists summon us to thriving. Their performances illustrate the best and worst of life, provoking dialogue, and creating life-affirming possibilities. They create meaningful disruptions, inviting us to see and live in new ways. They present enlivening alternatives, helping us confront injustices and look at relationships with fresh eyes. By celebrating beauty, novelty, improvisation, and experimentation artists cultivate conditions for thriving. There is much to be learned from the artists in our lives and from women who live life as a work of art.

The questions, stories, and practices in this chapter are invitations to dialogue about living life as a work of art.

It's as though there is a communal dreaming going on underneath everything, a great river of co-creation where our individual dreams, our individual lives touch and are touched by the dreams of others, and that is how our common world is made.

Joan Sutherland, Roshi

12-1. CREATIVITY ON THE EDGE

Innovation and creativity are found on the edges of life, the places that are uncertain, novel, often energizing, and sometimes chaotic. To make change, we need to be *edgewalkers*. In order to learn and grow, we need to be curious, to try new things, to disrupt life as usual, and to experiment with new ideas, places, and people.

1. Who and what are on the edges of your life right now? Maybe a provocative question, or an exotic place to visit, or a new art.

   » Why are these edgy things important to you?

   » Who are you with as you engage in these activities?

   » How are they encouraging you? Supporting you?

   » How do you feel when you are being edgy?

2. Tell me about an edgy question you are currently seeking to answer. What it is? What makes it edgy?

   » How does asking this question bring out your best?

   » How might the answer change your life? Other lives?

3. Tell me about a tradition or social norm that you are currently disrupting or wish to disrupt. What is the tradition or norm?

   » Why do you want to disrupt it?

   » What makes doing so edgy and innovative?

4. One big idea, if you could invent one thing that would make the world a better place for girls and women, what would it be?

12-2. CREATIVE SELF-EXPRESSION

We all express ourselves in different ways as we bring our values and strengths to life in service to the world. Some of us express our creativity through food, spices, and simmering pots. Others use words, paragraphs, and pages. Still others use movement, dance, and music. Whatever its form, our creative self-expression is essential for our well-being, influence, and success.

1. Tell me about a time when you felt free to express yourself. What was the situation?

   » Who or what enabled you to feel free?

   » What medium did you use to express yourself?

   » What did you say or do? How did others respond?

   » What was important about this for you?

2. Recall a time when you learned to express yourself in a new way, perhaps music, drawing, or giving a speech. What was it that you learned as a means of expression?

   » Who helped you? How did they encourage you?

   » How do you use this form of self-expression in your work?

   » How do you feel when you do this?

3. Imagine being invited to give a commencement speech. What do you tell graduates about the importance of finding their voices?

   » What would you say about having the courage to creatively express yourself?

   » What story from your own life would you share to illustrate the importance and benefits of creative self-expression?

☽ A Practice: Rip, Stick 'n' Chat

Margi Brown Ash & Leah Mercer

After many years working with theatre, collage, and arts therapies, we've developed *Rip, Stick 'n' Chat* as a way to generate creative ideas, to understand personal and relational patterns that could help or hinder connection and collaboration, and to unpack arising conflicts in a supportive, creative environment.

You need five things for *Rip, Stick 'n' Chat:* An open mind; an aesthetic environment; a pile of used magazines, brochures, postcards – anything that contains evocative images and text you're happy to rip apart; glue sticks; and paper for each participant.

Rip, Stick 'n' Chat is an exercise for engaging with what some call our unconscious, what we don't know we know. We rip and stick while we chat. The intention is to occupy our logical minds while allowing our imaginations the freedom to explore.

People sometimes want to start with a specific question or theme. That's okay, but experience has taught us that what we need to share and discuss will emerge from the process.

Step-by-Step Rip, Stick 'n' Chat

1. Collage Making

   » Surround yourself with who and what you need.

   » Give each person a piece of paper or two and a glue stick.

   » Invite everyone to rip out images and words that appeal to them and to glue them onto their piece of paper.

   » Have fun.

2. Post Collage Chat

   » With a partner take turns describing each collage.

   » Let the collage direct the conversation. Notice shapes, colors, textures, sizes, image placement, relationships between images, and what you see as missing. Discuss what surprises you. Celebrate what emerges from the seemingly accidental or unintentional placement of images. That's where the gold lies. Avoid interpretation.

   » As you share, write down words or phrases that arise from the conversation.

3. Stream of Consciousness Writing

   » Establish and share a time limit of 10, 15, or 20 minutes.

   » Sit quietly alone with pen and paper and reflect in writing.

   » Begin by writing: "What I really want to say is..."

   » Continue writing without lifting your pen off the paper.

   » If you get stuck, either rewrite the opening phrase, or write: "What I know is...," and keep going.

   » Remember to breathe as you write.

4. Post Writing Chat

   » Read your writing aloud, either a couple of lines or in full.

   » Have a conversation about what emerges. Focus on the strengths and discoveries and how you feel about them.

   » Notice how you've seamlessly moved from a description of the collage to new meaning. Share what surprises you.

   » Notice what you wrote that relates to being the best version of yourself right here and now.

   » Notice and share possible steps forward.

This playful approach to meaning-making can be used for people to explore their unique forms of self-expression and creative ways of thriving.

12-3. Silence, Life's Greatest Ally

As much as we need people, we also need time alone in reflection, meditation, mindfulness, and silence. This is especially the case for those of us juggling family, school, work, and care for others. The fuller our life becomes, the more essential it is to give ourselves empty time and space to relax, refresh, and renew. At these times, silence can be our greatest ally, giving us just what we need to connect with what is most meaningful to us.

1. Describe your relationship with silence. Where do you find it?
   » How often do you spend time in silence?
   » How does it call to you?
   » What does it feel like for you to be with silence?

2. Imagine a day of silence. Where would you be?
   » See yourself walking in nature, quietly appreciating beauty.
   » See yourself turning your face to the sun, relaxing.
   » See yourself making a meal and eating in silence.
   » How would you feel at the day's end?

3. Recognizing the importance of stillness, tell me how you create a routine of silence, meditation, or mindfulness.
   » Is it daily or weekly?
   » What do you do? For how long?
   » How do you feel after doing these things?

12-4. CELEBRATING MYSTERY

Mystery surrounds us in all places and in all we do. We call it by many names – muse, intuition, spirit, science, wisdom, uncertainty, the creator, or God. Whatever we call it, we know it as a life-affirming force for good. We find it in relationships, literature, and music. We meet it on walks in nature and in the midst of creative endeavors. We actively call it into our lives, our work, and our relationships through ceremony, ritual, and prayer.

1. Tell me about the ways you embrace mystery in your life. What do you call it?

   » Where and when do you encounter it?

   » Do you attempt to understand or control it?

   » How do you draw upon it for strength and courage?

   » How do you invite it into your life?

2. Share a story about moment of synchronicity, a time when the mystery of life gave you just what you needed at just the right time. What happened?

   » Who else was involved? What did they do or say?

   » What did this moment enable for you? For others?

3. Imagine you have been asleep for a long time. As you awake, you see that things are very different around you. What you see is a society guided by mystery rather than rules and roles.

   » What sights and sounds do you notice?

   » How are people interacting?

   » What has changed for the better for women and girls?

   » Now you realize that you were not sleeping, but rather you helped make this society possible. What did you do?

Beyond Gendered Spirituality

by Joy Mills

Forty years ago, in an instant, my understanding of my life as a woman changed. During a church service, I heard women's names proclaimed along with the long-established list of Our Fathers: "God of our fathers and mothers, God of Abraham and Sarah, Isaac and Rebecca, Jacob and Rachel." Even though I had never felt excluded in the church's rituals, in a blaze of recognition, I knew I had never been included. This moment of radical spirituality was a visceral awakening, mirroring a rejoicing of my soul and opening me to a spirituality that continues to transcend the male-gendered faith I had imbibed since childhood.

Propelled by this moment, during church services I quietly changed the masculine words addressing G*d as well as people. To work toward expanding the church's images and language, I was called to the Episcopal priesthood. Discovering the necessity of deep inner work to release male-dominant patterns, I studied psychology as well as theology to understand the long-term impact of male G*d language on women and men. My seminary nurtured the exploration of the intersection of racism, sexism, capitalism, all systems which support one group's power over other groups. I brought together the masculine and feminine energies by praying to Yahweh-Shekinah, Jesus-Sophia, Ruach-Spirit. As a priest, I included Hagar, other wife of Abraham, and Leah, first wife of Jacob, then added the names of independent women such as Deborah, Judith, and Esther.

My theology shifted to raise up the relational, empowering, loving aspects of my Judaeo-Christian heritage and to reject its death-dealing aspects, an opportunity available for all faith expressions. The accelerated desecration of the Earth, the #MeToo movement, and climate change focus the intersection of our spirituality on systemic issues. How does our spirituality engage with the fact that one in three women will be assaulted during their lifetimes? That even as they seek sanctuary, immigrants fleeing poverty and oppression have become disposable? That trees, open space, and minimum wage earners with their children have become expendable to feed human greed?

Now I consciously stand on Earth Mother, reaching toward Sky Father, with reverence for Grandmother Ocean Water, in the presence of Grandfather Fire listening with gratitude for the wisdom of the Four Elements which sustain us. I listen to the Great Spirits of the Four Directions. I take action because I believe these energies hold all people responsible.

No longer is a private faith dominated by demanding male images and exclusively male language. This fluid spirituality is inclusive, empowering, and expansive. It echoes the stories of faith-seekers around the world who are listening and responding to an abundant spirituality. As it transcends our individual interests, it embraces the life-giving essences of our traditions. Fluid spirituality longs for us to hear and participate in the groaning of the Creation crying out for a renewed, compassionate, and loving world.

12-5. Living with Purpose

We are at our best when we live with purpose, using our strengths in service to a better world. Some of us seem to know our life purpose from an early age. Others wonder for years, "Why am I here? What am I meant to do?" Our most meaningful purpose can be found at the intersection of our strengths, wisdom, and capabilities with the world's greatest needs. We live our life with purpose when we dedicate our best selves in service to a better world.

1. Tell me about a time when you felt you were living with purpose in a project or for a day. What were you doing?

    » Who else was involved?

    » What were the outcomes of what you did?

    » What about this situation gave you a sense of purpose?

2. Think about the patterns in your life. What activities do you do, repeatedly, over and over?

    » What do you do weekly? Monthly? Every year?

    » Who do you do these things with? For?

    » What do these patterns tell you about what is most meaningful to you?

3. Tell me your biggest and boldest dream for a better world. Why does this matter to you?

    » What one thing can you do to realize this dream?

    » What support do you need?

    » How will you get it?

    » How will you celebrate little steps along the way?

12-6. KEYS TO OUR WELL-BEING

Each of us has a short list of keys to our well-being, those 5 to 7 aspects of life that support our thriving. They include things like, exercise, continuous learning, travel, friends, making art, or singing. Knowing and living in alignment with our own keys to well-being enables us to be our best and make a positive difference in the world.

1. Think about a time when you were at your best, successful, and feeling a sense of well-being. What was the situation?

   » What were you doing that made it a special time?

   » How did others contribute to your well-being?

   » What were some of the conditions that brought out your best in this situation?

   » What does this story tell you are your keys to well-being?

2. Describe a woman whose well-being is apparent.

   » What does she do to support her own well-being?

   » What would you say are the keys to her well-being?

   » What is it like to be around her?

3. How have the keys to your well-being changed over your life?

   » How did you know it was time for a change?

   » What did you do to make the change?

   » What needs to change in your life now?

   » How might you make this change?

12-7. Grief, a Bittersweet Emotion

In the course of life, we must sometimes let go of cherished people, animal companions, and ways of being. With letting go comes grief, the bittersweet combination of loss with remembered joy. Grieving is a process with its own rhythm of denial, anger, and sadness. It is sacred work, honoring relationships that have passed and the universal flow of life and death.

1. What is your relationship with grief? Has it been a constant companion in life or a recent visitor?

2. Tell me about an experience of grief in your life. Who or what passed from your life?

   » How were you supported in your grieving?

   » What support did you find most meaningful?

3. Grieving varies across cultures, societies, and families. What are your family's ceremonies and rituals for grieving and supporting people experiencing grief?

   » How do you know support is needed?

   » What do you say or do?

4. Imagine now a world with spaces and rituals for grieving, a world in which grieving and related emotions are honored, and people who are grieving are cared for. What would this world look like, sound like, and feel like?

12-8. Wise Women, Wise Ways

Wisdom derives from many sources. Self-reflection, open and transparent communication, contemplation, and diverse personal experiences all prompt the cultivation of wisdom. Wise women listen attentively, hold space for others to be themselves, and live with respect for all life. They measure success in terms of well-being, peace, and harmony, not just power and profit.

1. Tell me about a wise woman in your life. How are you related?

    » What wisdom have they shared with you? When?

    » How do you feel in their presence?

    » How do they cultivate wisdom?

    » How has their wisdom helped you be who you are today?

2. Recall a time when you felt wise. What was the situation?

    » How did you express or demonstrate wisdom?

    » How did relationships change in the presence of wisdom?

    » How do people look, sound, and feel in the presence of wisdom?

    » How do you actively cultivate wisdom?

3. Imagine a conversation with your younger self. What would you like to tell her? What wisdom would you share with her?

Wise people, studies show, are especially discerning because they are able to see holistically and integrate seemingly contradictory perspectives to achieve balance and well-being in everyday life.

Barbara Fredrickson

12-9. UNCONDITIONAL LOVING

A thriving world is a world no longer divided by gender violence, abuse, and injustice; but is instead a world deeply connected by unconditional love that honors differences. To be accepted just as we are is a great gift. Whether from a parent, child, partner, best friend, or God, unconditional love is a wonderous source of healing, happiness, and wholeness.

1. Recall a time when you experienced unconditional love. Who else was involved?

   » Where was this? What was the situation?

   » How did unconditional love affect you? Others involved?

2. Share a story about a person or a relationship that was healed or restored by love. How does it feel to tell this story?

3. Tell me about a time when someone's unconditional acceptance of you helped you claim and celebrate a part of yourself that you had forgotten. What was the situation?

   » What did they do or say?

   » What did you recall about yourself?

   » How have you changed as a result of this experience?

4. Tell me about a time when you felt unconditional love for another person or the world. What led you to this?

   » How did you express your feelings at the time?

   » How did this experience positively affect others? You?

   » What might you do to have more of this in your life?

12-10. Relational Legacy

Our legacy is the stories people tell about us, about what we have done in our lifetime, about the kind of person we are, and about the relationships we cherished and nurtured. We live and will be remembered by what we do, the kindness we share, and the relationships we have with all of life. Our relational legacy lives on in what we do to sustain the world for all our relations.

1. Who are the people for whom you wish a better world? What are your hopes and dreams for them?

   » How have you organized your life to realize these hopes and dreams?

   » What are you most proud of having done that will endure as your legacy?

2. What have you done to keep your relationships in good order?

   » In what ways have you nurtured relationships?

   » What have you done to keep them strong and healthy?

   » How have you rebalanced things when relationships went askew?

3. Imagine that people have gathered to remember and celebrate you. Perhaps a special award, an 80th birthday, a retirement, or a memorial service.

   » What stories do you hope they will be telling about you?

   » What are you proud about? What makes you feel as if you have left a valuable legacy?

4. What one thing can you do today to contribute to this generative legacy you have imagined?

What the World Needs Now

by Judy Rodgers and Gayatri Naraine

Love is natural and innate in each human soul. To be loved is the seed of happiness. To give love to others is the source of our fortune. Love wells up from the depths of a soul, unless the soul has been so harmed that anger and sorrow are blocking love like a cloud in front of the sun. When this is the case, the healing for that soul comes from receiving the sustenance of pure, unconditional love.

When we are in the awareness of our eternal nature as souls, we easily and naturally tap into a wellspring of love. The more we stabilize ourselves in sweet, internal silence by turning inwards, the more we experience unlimited love and are able to share love with others. Love has its own language. You might say it has three languages: of feelings, of thoughts, and of the eyes.

The language of feelings: *When we want to know the truth of how we feel, we can put our hands on our hearts and ask ourselves, "How am I?" The heart knows the truth about us. When we are centered in our true spiritual nature, the heart is at peace and is naturally loving.*

The heart harbors not only love, but also pain of accumulated memories and disappointments. Disheartenment is literally to have dis-ease in the heart. It is not our deepest truth, but the energies of sadness, fear, anxiety, and anger can eclipse our inner light, can block our access to our innate loving nature. When this happens, we can't share pure love with anyone.

We need to clear the heart of the vestiges of the past that keep us separated from our true loving nature. This inner work is done in solitude or in connection with God. Once the heart is clear, peace and spiritual love naturally fill the heart, and we serve through the pure feelings flowing from our hearts towards everyone.

The language of thoughts: *To have pure feelings means to have* *powerful thoughts. Faster than all the instruments of science is the speed of thought. When we have pure feelings for souls, it means that we have powerful, pure, and auspicious thoughts that there should be benefit for souls. When our thoughts and feelings harmonize, the souls we are serving will experience that they are receiving peace and power through special cooperation.*

To do this subtle service with thoughts, the mind has to be free of distraction. When we allow our thoughts to be busy with small matters, the inner pathway over which our most generous thoughts flow does not remain clear. For the language of thoughts to reach other souls, we need to make time for solitude, even if it is for one or two minutes. Even if the external situations are creating upheaval, the soul with habits of solitude will be able to concentrate rapidly by going into the depths of inner awareness.

The language of the eyes: *It is often said, "The eyes are the windows of the soul." When we're in a state of inner (soul consciousness) awareness, when our feelings are pure and our minds are clear, anyone who comes in front of us naturally experiences a wave of love coming from our eyes. In the mirror of love, they would experience being truly seen for who they are, perhaps after a long time. When we're in this inner awareness of our eternal, spiritual nature, there naturally would be the fragrance of spiritual love in the atmosphere around us. Now is the time that the world desperately needs this fragrance of love.*

The world is hungry for love. Having seen selfish love again and again, people's hearts are disillusioned. When they experience true spiritual love for even a few moments, they feel they have received real life support. This is the most subtle and powerful form of service we can do.

13
THE ARTS OF THRIVING

By practicing the arts of thriving, women accomplish their goals
and grow into the people they dream of being.

Writing this book has been a journey of profound wonder, connection, and collaboration. Shifting from #MeToo to Thriving Women, Thriving World taught us much about ourselves, about each other, and about the worlds we inhabit. Coming to understand thriving as a unique blend of success and developing well, we realized that we are all thriving women, each in our own gloriously different way. Remembering how significant education, self-sovereignty, and financial savvy are for women's success, we shared gratitude for our educations, our teachers, our parents, and our many learning partners. Writing reaffirmed our belief that the world thrives as women thrive. It reassured us that social transformation is possible, especially when women support women and when men support women leading positive change.

In the process of writing, talking, and sharing we uncovered five ways that women actively practice thriving. We call them the Arts of Thriving. Each one contributes to our abilities to both succeed and develop well, to achieve our goals while maintaining what Buddhists call "right relationship," and to use our life experiences to grow into the best versions of our unique selves.

Our best self is the greatest gift we can give the world.

CURATING LIFE-AFFIRMING STORIES

Thriving women practice the art curating life-affirming stories. They invite, share and celebrate stories. In the way water surrounds fish and is essential to their lives, we live and become in stories.

We are born into the stories of our families, our cultures, and our ancestors. We live into these inherited narratives, we adopt some, we fight with some, and we outright reject others. We pass on stories to help others learn and to share what we know. We are held and remembered in stories.

Stories grant meaning to our lives, our relationships, and our work. They can enable us or disable us, lift us up or pull us down, include us or exclude us, give us power or give it to others. We live and become in the spaces and potentials stories offer us.

For these reasons, thriving women don't surround themselves with just any stories. We wrap ourselves and others with positive life-affirming stories, with stories aligned with our values, dreams, and goals, and with noble stories of successful people creating a thriving world.

Creating Meaningful Disruptions

Thriving women practice the art of meaningful disruption. Social change requires disruption in the norms, social patterns, and relational realities of the prevailing cultures into which we are born and expected to take our places. Thriving is an invitation to be a social pioneer, a pattern breaker. It is a call to live in ways that make the world a better place now and for future generations. It is a summons to create meaningful disruptions that align our ways of living and working with core values and preferred futures, to liberate women and girls from oppression and exploitation, and to create positive ripples of social change for years to come.

The potential for disruption signals us. When interrupted as we talk, when touched inappropriately, when we hear mean or belittling comments about women, we pause. In these moments invisible social grids awaken us, and opportunities for disruption appear. In these moments we have a choice, to ignore what we see, or to name it, point out injustice, and make change even at a great cost because the value of change is much greater than the cost.

Meaningful disruptions become the times we look back upon and say 'I did it,' 'We did it,' 'We made a difference'. No matter how small or large, meaningful disruptions can soothe relational wounds, uplift new possibilities, and restore dignity to those from whom it has been taken. As thriving women, we give voice to our values and speak up for social justice. By working toward harmony in place of divisiveness, we create conditions for love and respect to prevail and sustain us all.

Caretaking Generative Relationships

Thriving women balance caring for others with caring for themselves. In most cultures, it has been, and still is, a woman's role to take care of others. The front-line roles of caretaking others in education, healthcare, nonprofit, and social services are still predominantly occupied by women. Although this may be a lamentable snapshot of inequality, it also invites us to consider women as purveyors of a relational savvy of great social value. Women in our thriving moments leverage this aptitude to take care of ourselves and others in healthy ways. The people around us form precious memories of being taken care of when it mattered most.

As we seek to bring balance and harmony into our lives, we learn to discern and say no to unhealthy relationships: those with people that take more than they give, drain our energy, deny our presence, or harm us in any way. At the same time, we seek out and support healthy relationships: those with people who bring out our best, encourage us to live and lead from our hearts and minds, and provide support and caretaking in return. Thriving women are caretakers of generative relationships in partnership with allies who uplift and energize us to lead the way.

Celebrating Strengths and Successes

Thriving is a lifelong dedication, a choice to live and work in ways that energize, embody, and uplift individual and collective best selves. Thriving women celebrate their own and others' strengths and successes as they are discovered and made meaningful through dialogue. By celebrating our strengths and successes we locate ourselves in the center of our own unique and meaningful lives. Appreciation, recognition, and celebrations give definition to our best selves, remind us of our values, help us calibrate how well we are doing, and inspire us to keep going.

Thriving women recognize, enjoy, and celebrate differences among people. Most significantly, we acknowledge and appreciate thriving. We support and applaud other women who are successfully doing what is in the best interest of people and the environment. We cheer on women doing something they have never done before. We share stories and best practices of how we take care of ourselves when we come face to face with oppressions, injustice, or relational abuse. We celebrate women and men who chart new pathways of gender equality at home and at work. By remembering and celebrating thriving moments, we create the bedrock upon which a thriving world is built.

Cultivating Conditions for Thriving

Thriving happens in part by chance, in part by choice, and in part by conditions that foster well-being and bring out the best of people. Conditions such as leadership, laws, regulations, access to time, money, and resources, organization cultures, and relationship norms can all contribute to oppressive, exploitive, and unjust environments, or they can contribute to a fertile milieu for thriving.

As Winston Churchill reminded us, "First we design our structures and then they design us." Thriving women give form and transform the conditions of our lives. We design laws, communities, and economic policies, so that thriving is inevitable. Much like gardening, thriving women sow the seeds of inclusion, equality, and collaboration and weed out injustice and abuse, cultivating a social environment of equality, peace, and harmony.

Epilogue

by Diana Whitney

Writing this book has been a labor of love, a time of untamed questioning, profound listening, deep learning, and casting off beliefs and assumptions that no longer serve the people. I am honored to be, in the words of my Lakota relatives, "the hollow bone" through which the promise of this book has come to life.

While writing, I endeavored to hold the ideas and ideals of my coauthors with a loving heart and a gentle hand. As a bouquet of delicate flowers, some blossomed forth on the pages of this book, while others wilted and were left behind during the book's many iterations. Thank you for understanding.

With love, I thank all of you, coauthors and contributors, family, friends, and colleagues, who have been on the journey from #MeToo to Thriving Women, Thriving World with me from the start. Special thanks to Amanda Trosten-Bloom whose selfless reading and revisions added clarity to many of the books' pages! To Dawn Dole who masterfully guided this book from start to finish, thank you for your magical balance of flexibility and focus. To my cofounders of the Taos Institute, Mary Gergen, Ken Gergen, Sheila McNamee, Harlene Anderson, and David Cooperrider, thank you all for so elegantly articulating practices for peaceful, relational worlds through your writing, teaching, and speaking. This book is a bold experiment, applying the appreciative, collaborative, constructionist, and future-forming ideals we share to one of society's most pressing issues, women's equality and liberation. I am delighted that this book is a Taos Institute publication.

I offer a prayer of loving kindness to all who have come before us, to all who are with us now, and to all who are still to join us on this journey to a thriving world.

Author Biographies

Diana Whitney, Ph.D., is an internationally acclaimed consultant, writer, and inspirational speaker working at the forefront of the fields of dialogical organization development and positive social change. She is an expert in Appreciative Inquiry and Appreciative Leadership, an executive advisor, founder of Corporation for Positive Change and co-founder of the Taos Institute. She is an award-winning author of twenty books including *The Power of Appreciative Inquiry* and *Appreciative Leadership.* diana@positivechange.org

Kathryn Britton, MAPP, is an executive coach who works with technology managers, leaders, and creative writers. Her coaching is shaped by her leadership experience in software engineering, work with over 100 authors, and the study of positive psychology. She has published four books, including *Character Strengths Matter*, and numerous chapters and articles. kathryn@theano-coaching.com

Jessica Cocciolone, CFRE, serves as the Director of Development for Elk Hill, a statewide non-profit. She has fundraised for organizations across the United States, building shared visions and engagement opportunities for all stakeholders. Prior to Elk Hill, Jessica worked with High Achievement's national fundraising program, training market development officers on best practices and shared agendas for building a collaborative development program. jcocciolone1@icloud.com

Alejandra León de la Barra is a practitioner in Positive Psychology, specializing in Appreciative Inquiry with an MA in Positive Leadership from the Tecmilenio University in Mexico and MFA from the University of Iowa. Founder of the consulting firm, Appreciative Acting for Your Best Stage of Life, she works with parents, artist, teachers, and volunteers to help them increase their well-being using character strengths and gifts. alejandraleondelabarra6@gmail.com

Angela B. Koh, DMA, is a co-founder of Canadian Centre for Brief Coaching and a leading expert in the Solution Focused approach to workplace learning solutions. She works with clients across sectors. As a former concert artist, Dr. Koh believes in the creative potential of each and every client. angela.koh@briefcoaching.ca

Caroline Adams Miller is a leading expert on the science behind successful goal setting and the use of 'good grit' to achieve hard things. A Harvard graduate with a Masters in Applied Positive Psychology from the University of Pennsylvania, she has authored six books including *Creating Your Best Life* and *Getting Grit*. She teaches goals and grit at the Wharton Business School. caroline@carolinemiller.com

Haesun Moon is a passionate educator who specializes in transforming dialogues and social change. Her academic research at the University of Toronto introduced a simple coaching model, Dialogic Orientation Quadrant, that has transformed the way people coach and learn coaching. Haesun teaches Brief Coaching at the University of Toronto and serves as Executive Director at the Canadian Centre for Brief Coaching. haesun.moon@briefcoaching.ca

Marlene Wendy Ogawa facilitates innovative learning interventions across Southern Africa in private, government, and civil society organizations. She works with leaders and communities at Synergos Institute focusing upon poverty alleviation through social connectedness. Her Appreciative Inquiry practice has a special focus on gender and race inclusion strategies that strengthen communities and institutions. mogawa182@gmail.com

Tanya Cruz Teller, MA, is a creative leader ensuring a diverse, equitable, and inclusive world by building thriving organizations. She has a Masters in International and Intercultural Management and is currently based in South Africa. Her most recent work focuses on inspiring inclusion and innovation with Appreciative Leadership. Tanya excels by combining participatory convening, coaching, technology, and social media to engage whole systems in integrating their internal wisdom with collective knowledge. tcruzteller@me.com

CONTRIBUTOR BIOGRAPHIES

Mary M. Gergen, Ph.D., is co-founder and board member of the Taos Institute, Professor Emerita of Psychology, Women's Studies Program, Penn State University, Brandywine PA. Her work is located at the intellectual convergence of feminist theory, postmodernist thought, and social constructionism. Her books include *Playing with Purpose* and *Paths to Positive Aging.* gv4@psu.edu

Margi Brown Ash, Ph.D., co-founder of the Nest Ensemble, is a performer, director, writer, and lecturer. Margi also counsels artists in 'selves-care' and Rituals of Practice. 4change@iinet.net.au

Erin Bad Hand is a Native poet from Taos, New Mexico. She received her MFA from the School of the Art Institute of Chicago. She resides on the island of Oahu with her family. nape_sica@hotmail.com

Saliha Bava, Ph.D., is a therapist, consultant, researcher, author, and a bonus mom in NYC. She designs and implements play-based, dialogic change processes with organization, community, family, learning, and research systems. drbava@gmail.com

Hannah Joy Bloom is a K-8 teacher in Denver, CO with degrees in piano performance, English literature, and choral education. hannahjoybloom@gmail.com

Ekta Bromley is an Organizational Development consultant. Her approach to facilitation, program, and curriculum development is dialogic, collaborative, and inclusive. ekta.bromley@gmail.com

Lizanne Corbit, M.A., L.P.C., is a heart warrior, soul nurturer, rebel poet, and midwife to the spirit. As a psychotherapist she helps people own their essence selves. lizannecorbit@gmail.com

Diane Farrell is a teacher of the Feldenkrais® Method, a former Assistant Principal Cellist with the San Francisco Symphony, and a student of Gerontology focused on cognitive health, advocacy, and end-of-life issues. dmfarrell@me.com

Kenneth J. Gergen, Ph.D., is co-founder and president of the Taos Institute, the Mustin Professor of Psychology at Swarthmore College. A major figure in the development of social constructionist theory, his books include *Toward a Theory of Social Transformation, Realities and Relationships,* and *Relational Being.* kgergen1@swarthmore.edu

Charles P. Gibbs, an Episcopal priest, visionary, peacebuilder, and poet, believes his most important contribution to a positive future is to support and advocate for women's leadership in all areas of human endeavor. cgibbs@revcharlesgibbs.net

Mark Greene writes and speaks extensively about men's issues. He is the author of *Remaking Manhood, The Little #MeToo Book for Men* and co-author of *The Relational Book for Parenting.* mrkgreene@gmail.com

Kami Guildner helps clients raise up their voice, visibility and business to make the impact they want in the world. She is author of *Firedancer: Your Spiral Journey to a Life of Passion & Purpose* and host of the Extraordinary Women radio show. kami@kamiguildner.com

Medha Gupta is a 15-year-old Indian immigrant currently living in South Africa. This strongly influences her poetry.

Jordan Hackworth, MD, has previous publications primarily about Zofran use during pregnancy, though he briefly edited for The BickerBicker News. He lives in Charlottesville, VA.

Ginny Hanson is the founder of Sak Saum, Saang District of Cambodia. info@saksaum.com

Kay Lindahl is founder of The Listening Center, author of the award-winning book, *The Sacred Art of Listening*, and co-founder of Women of Spirit and Faith. Thelisteningcenter@yahoo.com

Rita Anita Linger, Ph.D., is an integrative health professional, organization development consultant and social justice advocate honored with her name and picture on a quilt, in the DeWitt History Museum, next to Dorothy Cotton, aide to MLK. zensister@gmail.com

Leah Mercer, co-founder of the Nest Ensemble, is an associate professor, theatre director, writer, and creative practice researcher in Theatre Arts at Curtin University, Australia. leahmerc@ozemail.com.au

Joy Mills a retired Episcopal priest and pastoral psychotherapist, treasures the opportunity to write about Fluid Spirituality as well as gathering people for ritual and conversation. joymills9@gmail.com

Gayatri Naraine, Brahma Kumaris UN representative, has dedicated her life to studying Raja Yoga and the spiritual dimensions of personal development. Gayatri.naraine@us.brahmakumaris.org

Elaine O'Brien, Ph.D., MAPP, is a pioneer in Fitness Science, and a visionary propelling dance and exercise for healing, learning, flow, and flourishing. positivefitlab@gmail.com

Shannon Polly, MAPP. Shannon's mission in life is to unleash the potential in her clients. She has trained over 1,500 Army sergeants in resilience. She co-edited *Character Strengths Matter.* Shannon@shannonpolly.com

Daniel Richardsson, Principal with Styrkebaserad i Sverige AB is an organization consultant and change maker in Sustainable Development, Flourishing Businesses and Societies. daniel@styrkebaserad.org

Judy Rodgers has studied Raja Yoga with the Brahma Kumaris for over twenty years and lives in a retreat center in the Catskill Mountains in New York. judyrodgers@gmail.com

Marian Franson Scott (1923-2011) was an art historian, world traveler, and exquisite friend. http://tinyurl.com/MarianLaura

Puno Selesho is a spoken word artist and a future social entrepreneur, residing in Pretoria, South Africa. She lives for three things, namely: God, Words, and People.

Amanda Trosten-Bloom, MSc, Principal of Corporation for Positive Change, is an international consultant and author in the fields of Appreciative Inquiry and positive change. amanda@positivechange.org

Maria Giovanna Vianello is Global Senior Organization Development Leader at Novartis for culture change, leadership development, and performance enhancement. maria_giovanna.vianello@novartis.com

END NOTES

Chapter 3: Thriving Women at their Best

Question 3-6 builds on a concept introduced by David Augsburger in his book, *Caring Enough to Confront*.

Chapter 6: Educating for Social Change

Angela Koh's piece, How We Build Confidence, references the research on growth mindsets by Carol Dweck and colleagues.

Chapter 8: Working for the Greater Good

Introduction: The quotation from Representative Ayanna Pressley appears in an article in Politico by Ruairí Arrieta-Kenna about the new women in Congress.

Chapter 9: Women Supporting Women

Question 9-6 draws from research on the Michelangelo Effect described by Sara Eckel.

Question 9-8 references the moais of Okinawa that are described by Dan Buettner.

Chapter 12: Living Life as a Work of Art

Question 12-1 uses the concept of edgewalkers described by Judi Neal.

References

Akashinga ("The Brave Ones"). (n.d.). *Nature protected by women.* Retrieved from https://www.iapf.org/akashinga/

Allee, V., & Chandra, D. (Eds.). (2004). *What is true wealth?* New Delhi: Indigo Press.

Aristotle. (n.d.). *Politics.* (H. Rackham, Trans.) Loeb Classical Library, No. 264.

Arrieta-Kenna, R. (2019, January 18). 'We call ourselves the badasses': Meet the new women of Congress. *Politico.*

Augsburger, D. (1973, 2018). *Caring enough to confront: How to transform conflict with compassion and grace.* Grand Rapids, MI: Revell.

Bava, S. (2016). Making of a spiritual/religious hyperlinked identity. In D. Bidwell (Ed.), *Spirituality, social construction and relational processes: Essays and reflections* (pp. 1-17). Chagrin Falls, OH: Taos Institute.

Bava, S. (2017). Creativity in couple and family therapy. In J. L. Lebow, A. L. Chambers, & D. C. Breunlin (Eds.), *Encyclopedia of couple and family therapy.* New York: Springer.

Bava, S. (2019). Hyperlinked identity: A generative resource in a divisive world. In M. McGoldrick, & K. Hardy (Eds.), *Re-visioning family therapy.* New York: The Guilford Press.

Beard, M. (2017). *Women & power.* New York: Liveright Publishing.

Billan, R., & Humber, T. (2018). *The tallest poppy: Successful women pay a high price for success.* Canadian HR Reporter and Thomson Reuters Canada Limited. Retrieved from http://tinyurl.com/TallPoppyReport

Brown, D. J., Arnold, R., Fletcher, D., & Standage, M. (2017). Human thriving: A conceptual debate and literature review. *European Psychologist, 22*, 167-179. doi:10.1027/1016-9040/a000294

Buettner, D. (2012). *The blue zones: 9 lessons for living longer from the people who've live the longest* (2nd ed.). National Geographic.

Carter, J. E. (2009, July 14). Losing my religion for equality. *The Sydney Morning Herald*. Retrieved from https://tinyurl.com/CarterLetter

Chittister, J. (1995). *In a high spiritual season.* Women's Wisdom.

Clerkin, C. (2017). *What women want – and why you want women – in the workplace.* Greensboro, NC: Center for Creative Leadership.

Corbit, L. (2019). *Notorious poetic travels of the fierce feminine.* Cloverdale, CA: Temenos Publishing.

Crenshaw, K. (1991). Mapping the margins: Intersectionality, identity politics, and violence against women of color. *Stanford Law Review, 43*(6), 1241-1299. Retrieved from http://tinyurl.com/Margins-Intersectionality

Dweck, C. S. (2016). *Mindset: The new psychology of success* (Updated edition ed.). New York: Penguin Random House.

Eckel, S. (2019). The Michelangelo effect: Your relationship can be a tool that brings out the best in you. *Psychology Today*.

Eisler, R. (1995). *Sacred pleasure.* San Francisco: HarperSanFrancisco.

Ensler, E. (1998). *The vagina monologues.* New York: Villard.

Ernst & Young. (2013). *Women: The next emerging market.* Retrieved from https://tinyurl.com/EYWomenEM

Fredrickson, B. L. (2013). *Love 2.0: How our supreme emotion affects everything we feel, think, do, and become.* New York: Hudson Street Press.

Gergen, K. J. (1999). *An invitation to social construction.* London: SAGE Publications.

Gergen, K. J. (2009). *Relational being: Beyond self and community.* New York: Oxford University Press.

Gergen, M. M., & Gergen, K. J. (2012). *Playing with purpose: Adventures in performative social science.* New York: Taylor & Francis.

Gibbs, C. P. (2015). *Light reading: Poems from a pilgrim journey.* Charleston, SC: CreateSpace Independent Publishing.

Ginsburg, R. B. (2018, January 22). Justice Ruth Bader Ginsburg reflects on the #MeToo movement: 'It's about time'. (N. Totenburg, Interviewer) National Public Radio. Retrieved from https://tinyurl.com/Ginsburg-Totenburg

Glasspool, M. D. (2012). Remembrance, witness and action. In K. Schaaf, K. Lindahl, K. S. Hurty, & G. Cheen (Eds.), *Women, spirituality, and transformative leadership.* Woodstock, VT: Skylight Paths.

Goldberg, N. (2016). *Writing down the bones: Freeing the writer within* (Thirtieth Anniversary Edition ed.). Boulder, CO: Shambhala Publications.

Guerrilla Girls. (1985-2018). *Our Story.* Retrieved from https://www.guerrillagirls.com/#open

Huffington, A. (2016). *Thrive: The third metric to redefining success and creating a life of well-being, wisdom, and wonder.* New York: Harmony Press.

JBS International, Inc. (2017). *Baseline Data Collection Report: CARE Rwanda Safe Schools for Girls (SS4G, PCTFI Cohort 3) and A Better Environment for Girls (BEE) Projects.* Retrieved from https://tinyurl.com/SS4G-BEE

Langer, E. J. (2009). *Counterclockwise: Mindful health and the power of possibility.* New York: Ballantine Books.

Levy, B. (1996). Improving memory in old age throug implicit self-stereotyping. *Journal of Personality and Social Psychology, 71*(6), 1092-1107. doi:10.1037/0022-3514.71.6.1092

Levy, B., Slade, M. D., Kunkel, S. R., & Kasl, S. V. (2002). Longevity increased by positive self-perceptions of aging. *Journal of Personality and Social Psychology, 83*(2), 261-270.

Lietaer, B. (2001). *The future of money: Creating new wealth, work, and a wiser world.* London: Random House.

Lindahl, K. (2001). *The sacred art of listening: Forty reflections for cultivating a spiritual practice.* Woodstock, VT: SkyLight Paths Publishing.

Livni, E. (2017, September 10). The complete guide to thriving, compiled by scientists. *Quartz.* Retrieved from https://qz.com/1073044/

Manne, K. (2018). *Down girl: The logic of misogyny.* New York: Oxford University Press.

McKinsey Global Institute. (2015). *How advancing women's equality can add $12 trillion to global growth.* McKinsey Global Report. Retrieved from https://tinyurl.com/women12trillion

Miller, C. A. (1988, 2013). *My name is Caroline.* Putnam Valley, NY: Cogent Publishing NY.

Miller, C. A. (2009). *Creating your best life: The ultimate life list guide.* New York: Sterling.

Miller, C. A. (2013). *Positively Caroline: How I beat bulimia for good... and found real happiness.* Putnam Valley, NY: Cogent Publishing NY.

Miller, C. A. (2017). *Getting grit: The evidence-based approach to cultivating passon, perseverance, and purpose.* Boulder, CO: Sounds True.

Myers, D. D. (2008). *Why women should rule the world.* New York: HarperCollins.

Neal, J. (2006). *Edgewalkers: People and organizations that take risks, build bridges, and break new ground.* Westport, CT: Praeger Publishers.

O'Donohue, J. (2003). *The invisible embrace of beauty: Rediscovering the true sources of compassion, serenity, and hope.* New York: Harper Perennial.

Roosevelt, E. (1960, 2010). *You learn by living: Eleven keys for a more fulfilling life.* (Fiftieth Anniversary ed.). New York: Harper Perennial.

Sanchez, A. L. (2017). *The four sacred gifts: Indigeneous wisdom for modern times.* New York: Enliven Books.

Sengupta, S. (2000, October 21). Jimmy Carter sadly turns back on national Baptist body. *New York Times.* Retrieved from https://www.nytimes.com/2000/10/21/us/carter-sadly-turns-back-on-national-baptist-body.html

Solnit, R. (2014). *Men explain things to me.* Chicago, IL: Haymarket Books.

Sutherland, J. (2019). This floating world. In *Awaken your heart and mind.* Boulder, CO: Lion's Roar.

Tippett, K. (2016). *Becoming wise: An inquiry into the mystery and art of living.* New York: Penguin Press.

Trent, T. (2015). *The girl who buried her dreams in a can.* Viking Books for Young Readers.

UNESCO. (2019). *Gender Equality in Education*. Retrieved from https://tinyurl.com/UNESCO-Gender-Equality

Wall Street Journal Editor. (2007, January 27). Saudi women and Bill Gates. *Wall Street Journal*. Retrieved from https://blogs.wsj.com/davos/2007/01/27/saudi-women-and-bill-gates/

Whitney, D., & Trosten-Bloom, A. (2003). *The power of Appreciative Inquiry: A practical guide to positive change* (2nd ed.). San Francisco, CA: Berrett-Koehler.

Whitney, D., Trosten-Bloom, A., & Rader, K. (2010). *Appreciative leadership: Focus on what works to drive winning performance and build a thriving organization.* New York: McGraw-Hill.

Whitney, D., Trosten-Bloom, A., Cherney, J., & Fry, R. (2004). *Appreciative team building: Positive questions to bring out the best of your team.* Lincoln, NE: iUniverse.

Women's Global Empowerment Fund. (n.d.). Retrieved from https://wgefund.org/

TAOS INSTITUTE PUBLICATIONS

See all the Taos Publications at
www.taosinstitute.net/taos-books-and-publications

Taos Tempo Series:
Collaborative Practices for Changing Times

Thriving Women Thriving World, (2019) by Diana Whitney, Jessica Cocciolone, Caroline Adams Miller, Haesun Moon, Kathryn Britton, Alejandra León De La Barra, Angela Koh, Tanya Cruz Teller, Marlene Ogawa

The Magic of Organizational Life, (2017) by Mette Vinther Larsen

Paths to Positive Aging: Dog Days with a Bone and Other Essays, (2017) by Mary Gergen and Kenneth J. Gergen

70Candles! Women Thriving in Their 8th Decade, (2015) by Jane Giddan and Ellen Cole (also available as an e-book)

U&ME: Communicating in Moments that Matter, New & Revised! (2014) by John Stewart (also available as an e-book)

Relational Leading: Practices for Dialogically Based Collaboration, (2013) by Lone Hersted and Kenneth J. Gergen (also available as an e-book)

Retiring But Not Shy: Feminist Psychologists Create their Post-Careers, (2012) edited by Ellen Cole and Mary Gergen (also available as an e-book)

Developing Relational Leadership: Resources for Developing Reflexive Organizational Practices, (2012) by Carsten Hornstrup, Jesper Loehr-Petersen, Joergen Gjengedal Madsen, Thomas Johansen, Allan Vinther Jensen (also available as an e-book)

Practicing Relational Ethics in Organizations, (2012) by Gitte Haslebo and Maja Loua Haslebo

Healing Conversations Now: Enhance Relationships with Elders and Dying Loved Ones, (2011) by Joan Chadbourne and Tony Silbert

Riding the Current: How to Deal with the Daily Deluge of Data, (2010) by Madelyn Blair

Ordinary Life Therapy: Experiences from a Collaborative Systemic Practice, (2009) by Carina Håkansson

Mapping Dialogue: Essential Tools for Social Change, (2008) by Marianne "Mille" Bojer, Heiko Roehl, Mariane Knuth-Hollesen, and Colleen Magner

Positive Family Dynamics: Appreciative Inquiry Questions to Bring Out the Best in Families, (2008) by Dawn Cooperrider Dole, Jen Hetzel Silbert, Ada Jo Mann, and Diana Whitney

CPSIA information can be obtained
at www.ICGtesting.com
Printed in the USA
BVHW041715141219
566678BV00005B/150/P